My *Life* with *Mother Angelica*

Sister M. Raphael, PCPA

MY LIFE WITH MOTHER ANGELICA
SISTER M. RAPHAEL, PCPA

All rights reserved.
Copyright ©2015 by Our Lady of the Angels Monastery

No part of this book may be reproduced, stored in a retrieval
system, or transmitted in any form or by any means, electronic,
mechanical, photocopying, recording or otherwise, without the
prior consent of Our Lady of the Angels Monastery.

Second edition, first printing in USA
ISBN: 978-0-692-41901-4

To order copies, please contact
The Gift Shop of El Niño
www.nunsgiftshop.com
3224 County Road 548, Hanceville, AL 35077
(256) 352-0358

Book and cover design
Suzanne C. Hurtig, www.SuzanneHurtigDesign.com

This book is dedicated to
Mother M. Angelica,
who has been my friend, counselor,

companion, mother and guide.

It is written with gratitude to God

that in His Divine plan He

willed that she and I should live our

lives at the same time on earth.

Sister Raphael,
my friend + pal — Jesus loves
you + So do I —
Mother M. Angelica
7/21/86

CONTENTS

Mother Angelica and Sister Raphael with her artwork

CHAPTER ONE

Monastic Beginnings

"Isn't God good!" The words drifted through the parlor grill and black curtain. Immediately I glanced to an opening in the enclosure near the floor. It was large enough to allow me to see a woman's bare feet in a pair of bedraggled homemade sandals.

This was my first encounter with Sister Mary Angelica in the extern sisters' dining room of Sancta Clara Monastery, Canton, Ohio. The year was 1951, the month, January. I was a postulant of only a few days, having entered on the 13th, eight days after the Epiphany. Everything that happened in this house of God was an exciting experience for me. I had entered under the mistaken impression that I would never be permitted to see my parents and two sisters again in this world. My few visits to the Monastery had taken place in this room. With the opening of the curtained and grilled window, Mother Mary Clare would appear and draw back her black veil to see and talk with me. She had asked me to spend a few months on the public side of the building to help the sisters there, but I had come to be a cloistered nun. I was intensely curious about every glimpse I could have of life on the other side—the cloister.

At the time I entered, all I knew about the cloister was hearsay. Saint Francis of Assisi, along with St. Clare, founded the Franciscan Order of which I had become a member. I was to learn that the Church had sanctioned Religious Orders dedicated to the contemplative life—that is a life of prayer and union with God separated in a material way from worldly pursuits. The cloister is an area of the monastery building which is enclosed by walls, gates and by visitors' parlors which separate the nuns from their visitors by grilled windows and turntables through which articles may be passed. The purpose is to keep the noise and distraction of the world on the outside of the cloister so that those who have been chosen by God to keep their eyes on Him, may be free to spend their time in work and prayer. Specific times of prayer and community activities are prescribed by the rule of the Founder. Certain sisters volunteer or are designated to handle the visitors, shopping and telephone calls. These sisters are called extern sisters. Only by permission of the Abbess may any workman, plumber, carpenter, etc. enter the designated cloister. The nuns must have permission of the Abbess to leave this area whether for medical reasons or for those reasons deemed necessary by the Abbess. They may, however, go to those places which are designated as extern and intern areas where laypeople may be volunteering to help with certain work.

The special aim of our life is perpetual adoration of Jesus in the Blessed Sacrament, exposed for veneration on our altar. While the Blessed Sacrament is exposed, the nuns take hour-long turns in the Chapel for adoration.

Divine Office, the official prayer of the Church, is chanted by the nuns four times a day.

I was taking food out of the turntable the first time Sister M. Angelica spoke to me through the black curtain. "You're the new postulant!" I heard her say, "Isn't God good!"

It was to be three years before I would realize how profound an impact this beautiful sister would have on my life. By that time I would have my vows for a year and my name changed to Sister Mary Raphael. I adapted my unbridled spirit to the ways and disciplines of the monastic framework, but frequently my unrestrained laughter would burst upon the silence and ring through the halls.

My year as an extern postulant was over on April 1, 1952. I was taken into the cloister and introduced to all the nuns, whose voices, by then, I had come to recognize through the grilled parlor and turntables. It was an awesome experience. The Monastery was a rambling building attached to the old O'Dea mansion and opened onto the original gardens of the elderly couple. Mr. and Mrs. O'Dea had given their estate in Canton, Ohio to the Franciscan Nuns of the Most Blessed Sacrament in Cleveland, Ohio to become a chapel and monastery dedicated to Jesus in the Eucharist, exposed for public veneration. The formal gardens stretched toward a pavilion and ended in a wooded area where I was to spend many happy hours working and praying.

Canon law decrees that the Novitiate (the residence for young sisters) be situated in a separate part of the monastery away from the older community nuns. Postulants dressed in black for a year prepare for reception of the habit. Novices (in the brown habit and white veil) study the Rule of the Franciscan Order and prepare for their first vows—to live without property, in chastity and obedience—under the guidance of a Novice Mistress, especially chosen from among the community sisters with Solemn Vows.

When I entered the enclosure, the cloistered part of the monastery, I left the loving and joyful companionship of Sister M. Juliana and Sister M. Bernadette, the extern sisters, to find myself under the guidance and care of Mother M. Veronica, the Mother Mistress of Novices. She was a gentle person, deeply devoted to God and simple in her approach to prayer. With seven sisters I shared recreation and work, and with them, came to call her lovingly, "Mother Mystery." With her motherly counsels and good humor, I found a warm solace and soon overcame my loneliness for the extern sisters and the homesickness I felt for my family. The sound of our laughter and high spirits often filled the Novitiate halls.

The enclosure was a new experience for me. I was accustomed to all the freedom and activity proper to my modern upbringing. Suddenly, by God's Providence, I became a cloistered nun. I was like Alice in Wonderland, stepping through the looking glass and finding myself among the practices and customs of another age. Latin phrases were substituted for the usual greetings and expressions of gratitude. (It was explained that in preparation for my vow of poverty, nothing belonged to me anymore. All I had belonged to the community—myself included.) I was charmed by the quaintness of the wooden forks and spoons from which we ate, the basin and pitcher of water I found in my room for my morning "bath," and the homemade sandals of hemp and corduroy.

On the anniversary of St. Francis and Clare, we would abandon all restraint and dash about decorating the Novitiate with streamers of bright crepe paper, flowers and angel figures that I had painted and cut out to put on the walls. We often put on a play and acted out the life of the saint. At Christmas time, I painted angels and little children on the windows to brighten the Monastery. We sang Christmas carols for the community sisters and built a snowman in the courtyard for the sisters in the infirmary.

Every Holy Day of Obligation—Christmas, Easter, Pentecost, the Immaculate Conception—found us preparing special music and chants to celebrate at Mass. From Advent until Christmas the Monastery took on a special atmosphere of anticipation and fulfillment as we prepared for the coming of Jesus in the crib. Holy Week was a somber time as we sang the Gregorian chants, repeating the sighs of the ancient prophets from Lamentations of the Old Testament. Easter was exhilarating with its exultant Alleluias and Pentecost a triumphant time when we celebrated the coming of the Holy Spirit. To mark these special occasions, recreation was held in the community dining room and we had a chance to converse with the community sisters. Several times a year we had picnics in the woods when we would play volleyball and sing to the music of the accordion.

On November 7, 1953, I made my first vows and diligently followed the regulations of my new way of life, studying the lives of the saints and trying to understand how they had obtained the holiness which I felt was God's Will for me.

Suddenly, into my life burst Sister Mary Angelica, free, happy and full of the Love of Jesus. She had been sent to the Novitiate to give us an eight day retreat which was to change my life. By some miracle she had come through hardships inherent to the building of a new monastery and had become a spiritual giant through her devotion to God's Will.

My first experience of her spiritual guidance was a memorable one. I had no vocabulary with which to describe what was going on in my heart and so was not able to express myself. I sat entranced before Sister as she began to describe the humility of Jesus and the beauty of this God-Man for Whom we had given up all and Whose Life and Love we sought to imitate.

She made me realize that holiness is arrived at by following Him and that He loved me and wanted me to become His own. He was providing me opportunities to walk in His Footsteps. She let me see the deep love for Jesus that had made it possible for me to hang on to my vocation and had an air of assurance that told me her advice had endured the testing of the years and would work for me. As she talked, my fears dissolved and I was aware of being in the hands of one experienced at her trade. I knew my soul would be handled with gentle care and strong determination and that the sufferings in my life had been allowed by God to bring me to this moment. I caught her enthusiasm for our mutual vocation.

She wrote three resolutions for me that first week which still apply as I read them today from my note book:

1. *"My one thought, the ruling force in my life will be an ever increasing Love of Jesus by which each day I can attain another degree of Union."*

2. *"To accomplish this I will keep the eyes of my soul continually on Jesus, not in a forced way, but as one who lovingly looks at a beloved object."*

3. *"Virtue or fall, no matter, each will be an opportunity to sink deeper into the sanctuary where Jesus dwells alone and where we live together as if no one else existed in this world."*

The days sped by. I was happier than I ever knew I could be. Now I had a guiding light to follow and like the Bethlehem star, she was to lead me to the stable and crib where I would find my infant King.

As the days passed, Sister began giving me books on the spiritual life so that I could progress more deeply into the realm of prayer. Through my hands passed the writings of St. John of the Cross, St. Teresa of Avila, Paul of the Cross, St. Ignatius Loyola, St. Francis de Sales, St. Bernard of Clairvaux, Father Aerentaro, Brother Lawrence—all masters of the spiritual life. She also gave me books on the lives of the saints and how they had labored to become holy. I began to devour the Scriptures and as I did, the Holy Spirit poured His Love and Breath into my soul. Union with God became the desire of my life and contemplation the road that would lead me to it.

God was giving Sister Angelica light to probe deeply and understand the ways He chose to deal with souls. Her counsels were always inspiring and after a while I abandoned the books I was reading and began to write from memory all the directions she was giving me. My notes filled many books. The following are from my journals:

> *"Sister, what a wonderful thing for souls to love God—not to become saints, not to make others think they are holy, not for what God can give them, but to love God just because He is God and deserves our love.*
>
> *"If God found a soul who did that, don't you think He'd take care of everything for that soul in order for that soul to keep on loving Him? It's selfish to love God just for what He might give us."*

Mother Angelica's First Profession

CHAPTER TWO

The Suffering Servant

I began to notice about this time that Sister Angelica was limping and when I would tell her how much I could see Jesus in her eyes, she confided to me that the pain in her spine was almost unbearable. With an intense look on her face, she began to teach me how to deal with suffering.

"I try to embrace suffering all day long, whatever form it takes. Your will grows stronger and stronger. When impatient thoughts come, you can drive them out faster."

To encourage me, she gave the following account of some of her trials before and after entering the Monastery. Knowing her mother's great attachment for her, she realized it would be impossible to discuss her vocation or indicate any hint of her leaving home because her mother would be all alone. She arranged secretly to enter religious life. She sent a special delivery letter that would arrive at the same time her mother would be coming home from work. She made the sixty mile trip by bus to Cleveland, Ohio and was taken into the cloister. When her mother received the letter, she reacted in typical Italian fashion—hysteria. It was months before she was reconciled and came to visit her daughter.

Sister was not long in the enclosure before her knees began to swell from the hours of kneeling before the Blessed Sacrament. It became such a problem that the attention of the entire community was drawn to the fact that this postulant could not even make the necessary genuflections on entering the Chapel. Somehow the Mothers of the Chapter took this as an indication that she had no vocation and were considering sending her home. Sister did not understand what Our Lord was doing, but went on in faith.

The customary time for postulancy was six months, but because the Mothers doubted her vocation, her initiation lasted for nineteen. When the Chapter finally decided to send her home, Mother M. Clare spoke for her and offered to take her to a new foundation which was starting in Canton, Ohio—Sister's home town. Ordinarily sisters are not stationed so close to their families.

Accepting the decision as a manifestation of God's Will, Sister Angelica threw herself into the heavy work of starting a new foundation (monastery) in Canton. From the time she left the Cleveland Monastery, she never had trouble with her knees again. Our Lord had used this affliction to bring her to this new Monastery where she would have many trials and joys.

Community living was particularly hard for Sister Angelica. The contrast of various temperaments was magnified by the closeness and restrictions of cloistered life. Being impatient by nature, Sister had a constant struggle

BRACES AND WHEELCHAIRS

One day Sister Angelica explained to me the cause of her physical pain. She had fallen on a soapy floor while using a commercial scrubbing machine. The heavy cord had become tangled under the large brush and the machine, spinning wildly, flung her against the wall. The damage was not immediately apparent, but unknown to her a birth defect in her spine was becoming more and more aggravated and she was losing the use of her left leg. When she could no longer hide her pain, she told Mother M. Clare about it and was put in the hospital for observation.

Several methods were used to help the injured spine without operating. A body cast was put on and she was told to use crutches that were too long, in order to stretch the vertebrae. When the cast was removed, she was put into traction for six weeks. The traction was pulling the spine in the opposite direction of the curvature and because she was allergic to all pain killing drugs, there was no way to ease the intense pain. After four months in the hospital, when all these efforts failed, it was decided that a spinal fusion was necessary.

The night before the operation, the doctor made this announcement: "Sister Angelica, we're going to operate on your spine tomorrow. There's a fifty-fifty chance you'll never walk again, so in the morning, if you can't move your leg, don't be surprised. Good night." With that, he walked out, leaving behind him a panic-stricken nun who fled at once to the refuge of prayer. "Jesus," she pleaded, "if you let me walk again, I'll build you a monastery in the south." She didn't know why she said the south, but she made the promise in a night of panic and the bargain was struck. When the operation was performed, the doctor decided not to do the spinal fusion, but to remove an extra vertebrae and hopefully allow room for the spinal curvature to straighten out. There followed many tears, much pain, and a back and leg brace and crutch. The result was that she could not lift her foot without the use of a brace and her spine needed the support of a brace, which she still wears.

We watched Sister struggle bravely to walk again. And walk she did. There was much for Sister Joseph and me to do to take care of her and we vied with each other to try to make her comfortable. She endured everything so cheerfully that she gave courage to all who came to see her in the infirmary.

As she began to recover, Sister Angelica confided her promise to Mother M. Clare and received permission to pursue it when the time was right. She continued to guide the five sisters in her care. Suffering had deepened her capacity to love and understand souls. God was giving her light to understand the ways He chose to deal with us.

As we talked together, her dream began to unfold before me.

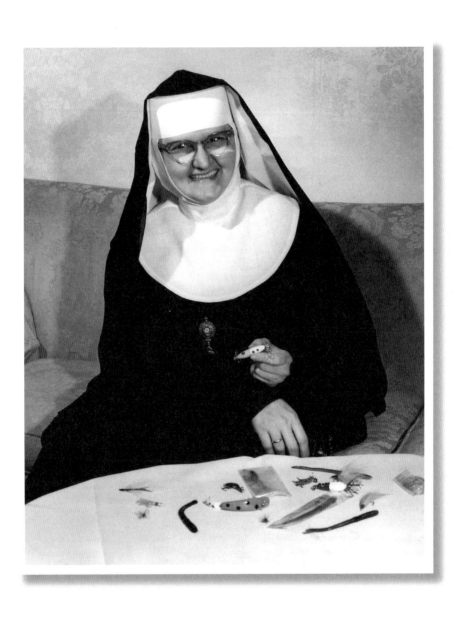

CHAPTER THREE

From Dreams to Vision
to Reality

"Someday we'll build our own monastery, Sister, where every sister's one desire will be to love Jesus and to grow in union with Him. We'll be one family and share everything in the manner of the early friars around St. Francis. It was not uncommon for them to tell each other what they had heard from the Lord and they all grew together in a caring family situation. I'll choose the sisters who will come to live there and train them in an atmosphere of love and family. I know we can have a monastery built on collegiality that would still be monastic." Prior to the Second Vatican Council monastic life was so structured that all decisions concerning the community were made by five or six council members who met with the Abbess each month. There was to be no class distinction in the monastery of her dreams, no separate group of councilors who knew everything and made all the decisions, no second choir sisters to do the manual labor while educated sisters were chanting the Office. (This practice developed in the old monasteries where girls were not educated and could not read the Latin Breviaries. First choir nuns chanted Divine Office while second choir nuns prepared meals etc.) Everyone would know all the joys and sorrows and pray together for all the intentions and needs of the community. We would not allow the community to grow so large that many rules would be necessary for its organization. These ideals were to coincide with those presented by Pope John XXIII during the Second Vatican Council. As the dream turned into a plan, Sister M. Joseph and I began thinking of ways to help support the community once it got established. Sister M. Joseph sewed altar linens and I was beginning to sketch faces of Jesus from different episodes of the Gospels.

Eventually Mother M. Veronica returned from Washington, D.C. and the tension was eased. I was soon to renew my vows and join the community sisters. When this happened, our plans for a new monastery in the south began in earnest. By this time, Sister Angelica had been elected to the council to advise the Mother Abbess on matters of finances, vocations, etc. and was given the title of Mother, along with the other five councilors. We were happy that now we were able to call her Mother in public since she had truly become a mother to us.

To found a new monastery, one must first find a bishop who is favorable to the idea of having cloistered nuns in his diocese. Contemplative life is not always understood and many wonder why we do not teach or nurse. Some of us feel called to give ourselves to God directly. Some bishops already have cloistered nuns, and others do not understand the importance of prayer. Canon law prescribes that the Abbess of a newly founded monastery be at least forty and her vicar thirty-five, so since Mother and I were both lacking in years we needed a special permission from Rome before we could leave the papal enclosure (the cloister).

Funds to support a new monastery are essential. While we were writing to bishops for necessary permissions and to Rome for permissions and transfers, we looked for means to raise funds. While rummaging through some magazines donated for the missions, Mother found her first lead in *Popular Mechanics*. She noticed an ad for making money by raising fishing worms. She approached Reverend Mother Veronica, who by this time had become Abbess after the death of Mother M. Clare. "Reverend Mother," she inquired innocently, "can I order a hundred earthworms? We can raise them in the basement and sell them to fishermen to raise money for the new foundation."

Mother Veronica shuddered. A basement crawling with worms was not her idea of a monastic occupation. She gave a gentle but firm refusal. Undaunted, Mother Angelica read further and came up with another idea. "We could order artificial lure parts, put them together and sell them to fishermen." Relieved that the project had advanced beyond live bait, Reverend Mother gave her consent and agreed to invest five dollars for a sample kit.

Upstairs in the laundry room, Mother Angelica hurried to tell Sister Joseph and me the exciting news that the lures had arrived. With dexterous fingers, the two began joining them and tying hooks while I encouraged, praised and applied band-aids to the newly hooked "fish." When the lures were assembled, we filled a bathtub with water and began pulling them around to see if they looked attractive enough to catch fish. Sister Joseph was the only one who had ever been fishing and she was delighted with the results.

One day a friend came to fix the refrigerator and happened to mention that he was going fishing that weekend. Mother disappeared down the hall and returned with the lures. "Try these, Bill, if they work we'll start making them."

"Where did you get these?" he exclaimed. "I paid a dollar and a half for a lure like this just last week."

Wheels began to turn in Mother's computer brain. She had paid only five dollars for the whole box. "Try them," she urged, "and let me know the results."

When the lures were enthusiastically endorsed a week later, Mother got permission to order more. She called a friend. "Cooney," she asked, "how can I sell a couple hundred fishing lures?"

"Easy," he replied. "I'll make up a brochure and give you a hundred dollars to buy a list of fishermen's addresses and we'll wait for the orders to pour in."

Two thousand brochures were stuffed into envelopes and after carefully attaching the labels, we took the bag of mail to the chapel to show to Jesus and ask His blessing on all the fishermen who answered. Then we waited. Eagerly we anticipated the huge response we would get with our first attempt to support our new Monastery. After all, it was for Jesus we had worked and prayed. From these 2,000 names we expected to hear from at least 1,999 fishermen. We would soon have the funds necessary to make our dream a reality.

Weeks went by and only two replies came in. As our dream faded, Mother Angelica and Jesus were not on speaking terms. "How can you do this?" she would say incredulously. "After all, it was for Him. I can't even look up at Him when I go in the Chapel."

Then it happened. Dale Francis, Editor of the Catholic Newspaper *Our Sunday Visitor,* sent an envelope on which was written "Marked Copy." He had been one of the fishermen and the idea intrigued him. In glowing terms, he told about the nun who would build a monastery with fishing lures. Mail began to pour in. We ordered more lures. More stories appeared in newspapers across the country and St. Peter's Fishing Lures were being promoted from coast to coast. We gave names to the lures like Wit's End, Little Mike, St. Raphael, Habakkuk, and St. Peter's Chains. Reports were drifting in from fishermen who had success with them.

One fisherman, who ordered one of each lure, responded

in a surprising way. In his print shop in Chicago, John Padlo laid out the lures on a blue background and made a four color photograph. A week later, a box of professional looking fishing lure brochures arrived and our excitement knew no bounds. With this professional mailing piece, orders increased and we scrupulously saved toward the monastery of our dreams.

It was around this time that the sisters expressed a desire to have a grotto for Our Lady behind the infirmary. Mother Angelica was asked to find men to do the work for us. After calling some of the leading churchgoers in the area and being refused, she got an inspiration. Remembering Mother Cabrini's work with immigrants in New Orleans, she began making phone calls. Her grandfather had provided a restaurant for Italian immigrants. She called one after another and not one refused. They were eager to do something for Our Lady.

"Are you sure you want guys like us to help you?" one of them asked with tears in his eyes.

"Yes" she said, "I'm going to ask Our Lady to get you all into heaven through the back door."

"How much do you want me to get from the boys?" another asked.

"I don't want money, I want men out here to pour and finish the concrete, lay stones and plant shrubs. I want a pedestal for Our Lady's statue to stand on. We'll make a scroll and Sister Raphael will letter all your names on it and we will cement it under the statue beneath Our Lady's feet."

And so they came, night after night until dark, working all summer pouring concrete and building the beautiful stone grotto that would house a marble statue of Our Lady the way she looked at fifteen years. Two stone planters made an "S" shape in front of this shrine, enclosing a patio where the sisters could come to pray.

As the grotto was taking shape, Mother expressed a desire

to have some hemlock trees behind the shrine and evergreen shrubs lining the flagstone approach.

"I know where to get some trees for you, Mother. I know a guy who has lots of trees," one of the men volunteered. She was about to express her gratitude when something in his voice stopped her.

"Where will you get them?" she asked.

"Me and the boys, we'll go up there on Saturday night. We can get all the trees and shrubs you want."

"Up where?" she asked in alarm.

"There's a guy north of here, he's got a lot of trees. He won't miss 'em."

"You can't just go there and take the man's trees. That's stealing. They don't belong to you."

"Trees belong to God," he countered. "This is God's house, so He can have His own trees, can't He? We'll take every other one, he'll never know they're gone." It was several more minutes before Mother convinced him she did not want the trees in that way.

CHAPTER FOUR

Dreams Become Reality

As long as I have known Mother Angelica, she has been in constant pain and hides the fact remarkably well. She describes how she deals with pain.

"To me, pain is a treasure. I have become accustomed to pain. Next to my vocation, it has been the cause of many graces. I know that on my own I can accomplish nothing. Pain makes me dependent on God for everything. It keeps me with Jesus. I can't do it without Him. It is a gift, a kind of security to keep me from becoming proud and arrogant or taking credit for what God is doing. I try to see Jesus and treat Jesus in everyone. I try to adapt myself to another's needs and personality. I try to understand the beauty and weakness in others so that they feel at home and free with me."

As winter came on, the cold weather caused her back and leg to go into spasms and she was often forced to retire early to relieve the pressure. One such night, in a vision, she saw on the wall above her bed a complete floor plan for the new monastery. She laid out some graph paper end to end on the bed and taped it together. This drawing was to become Our Lady of the

Angels Monastery in Birmingham, Alabama.

As word began to get around the house that a new foundation was being planned, another councilor decided she herself
would build one and since she had seniority over Mother
Angelica, indicated strongly that she should have first choice.

Reverend Mother Veronica was in a quandary. She knew
the sincerity and deep desire of Mother Angelica and the
promise she had made to God. We had already obtained permission from Bishop Walsh of Youngstown, Ohio, but had not
yet approached a bishop from another state to get permission
to erect a monastery in his diocese.

In desperation, Mother Veronica made a proposition with
God. Each of the two Mothers would write a separate bishop
for permission and mail the letters the same day. Whichever
responded first would be an indication of God's Will. We ago-
nized and prayed earnestly for three days.

"YA'LL COME"

It was Archbishop Thomas Toolen of the Mobile-Birmingham
Diocese who wrote those magic words, "Ya'll come!" The die
was cast. We were ecstatic.

People are seldom indifferent to Mother Angelica. Either
they recognize Jesus in her because the Holy Spirit is free within
them or the turmoil in their own soul blinds them and they feel
threatened, as was my own experience. I have never seen her
do anything selfish or degrading. Her one desire and goal is to
love Jesus and make Him loved. Her great joy is to spread His
message. Her eyes have a matchless beauty when she can witness to the fact that God uses the weak to confound the strong.
The whole effort of our apostolate is a witness to this truth.

From the floor plan that she had received from Our Lord,

Mother made a scale model of the building out of cardboard. From this, she made the electrical and plumbing plans. These she carried to Birmingham the first time she met with Archbishop Toolen and they were instrumental in convincing him that we needed to build, rather than live in an old house and try to turn it into a monastery.

The fishing lures were bringing in a continuous flow of money that we began saving to buy the land. The community at Canton had agreed to give us $50,000 to erect the building. In 1961, plans were made for Mother Veronica and Mother Angelica to leave the Canton cloister and look for land in Alabama.

During the three months it took to accomplish this, Mother Angelica was invited to speak before numerous and varied groups to explain our life and what the prayers of the nuns would mean to the city of Birmingham. At one such meeting with Jewish businessmen, she quipped, "I feel right at home here. You see, when I had my spinal operation, I wanted to see whose blood I was getting. As sick as I was, I squinted my eyes to read the names that were hanging upside-down on the transfusion bottles. The first one was Cohen, the second Luntz, and the third Goldberg. So I feel right at home in your presence."

After much traveling around Birmingham and praying, the property was found that fit our budget. In the suburb of Irondale, Mother found 15 acres of land for $13,000. This was the exact sum we had raised from the fishing lures. As they were driving away, she noticed a "For Sale" sign on a little house adjoining the property. After inquiring, she learned she could take up the payments and move in. It was an ideal place to stay while supervising the building and transacting business. Until this time she and her companion, Sister Joseph, had been staying with the Trinitarian Sisters. She likes to remark, "We came for dinner and stayed eight months!"

About this time, Mother and Sister Joseph were joined by

Mother's natural mother, Mae Francis, who left Canton, Ohio for Alabama and was considering becoming an extern sister once the monastery was built and the cloister established. She began cooking and entertaining the people who came to watch the building going up.

One day, Mother was told by the architect that she would have to sell the land. It sloped so drastically that the end result would be a sunken courtyard 50' x 80' x 20'. "This is the land the Lord gave us and this is where we build," was Mother's emphatic declaration.

"But," he argued, "you can't walk up one flight of stairs with your brace and crutch. How will you walk up those stairs?"

"We stay here," she repeated and just to be funny she added, "maybe somebody around here has a hill they don't want and we can pick it up and put it there."

As the building progressed and the walls went up, she saw what he meant. There was a HOLE—50' x 60' x 20'. One Saturday morning she was walking back and forth looking into it when she was joined by an old codger, chewing tobacco and spitting into the hole. "My God," she thought, "is he trying to fill that hole?" They walked silently back and forth and finally he made an observation. In a long, slow, Southern drawl he exclaimed, "Ya got a big hole there!"

"Yes, Sir," she agreed and then looking up to heaven at the Lord she whispered, "don't rub it in!" More walking, spitting and praying ensued and then another outburst.

"You need some dirt!"

"Yes, Sir," she answered, thinking to herself, "I need him like a hole in the head."

Finally the old man spun around with determination. "I've got a hill in back of my house. Every time it rains that damn thing's in my basement. You want it?"

"I want it, I want it!" she exclaimed. The next Monday

twenty tandem trucks brought that hill and dumped it into the courtyard. Somehow, while she was being facetious, the Lord passed by and said, "Amen."

The little house beside the property became the central office for transacting business, drinking coffee and eating spaghetti served by Mother Angelica's mother. People who came to watch the building progress went there to hear the stories told of early days of the order in Canton. Many friendships were formed which would endure through the years.

Into this atmosphere came an electrical contractor asking to speak to the supervisor. Mother Angelica had answered the door and replied, "I'm the supervisor." Looking embarrassed he asked for the contractor. "I'm the contractor," she said.

"Well, let me talk to someone who can read these plans."

"I'm the one," she said emphatically, "show them to me."

Exasperated he unrolled the plans and asked her to check them. "Like some miracle," Mother related later, "I saw one mistake at first glance." "Here's a mistake," she said. "This outlet is in the wrong place." Unbelieving, he quickly lowered his head to see better and then took a good look at Mother.

"My God, you're right," he said, and from that day he never questioned her authority again.

Pictures of Mother and her project began appearing in the newspaper and calls came in from people who wanted to be a part of this house of prayer. One man donated all the block, mortar, sand and concrete for the entire building. Another did all the blasting of rock and moving of fill dirt to level for the building and then returned her payment check to her on dedication day. All the brick was given by a young woman and her mother who owns a brickyard in town.

Mother was called to look at some floor tile one day that was being offered as a gift. "I don't think you understand, this is not a convent. This is a monastery. We have 11,000 sq. ft. of floor here to cover."

"That's what the paper said," he replied. "I want to give you the floor tile." She and Sister Joseph went over to his place of business and looked at the brown tile he wanted to donate. Mother thought it was a bit dark and as they left she said to Sister, "This Grecian Rose is pretty."

"Yes," replied Sister Joseph, "but that's not what he's giving you. Maybe we should pray about it." The next Monday when they returned from Mass, there were workmen in the building putting down the beautiful Grecian Rose tile. Mother called the donor and asked if there was some mistake.

"No," he said, "after you left I looked at the Rose tile and thought it would be a lot more cheerful than the brown."

One Saturday, after they had decided not to paint the inside of the building to save money, Mother called a paint store just to ask if they had anything left over from other jobs that she could get cheaper. "How much do you need, Mother?" the man asked. "About a hundred gallons," she told him off the top of her head. He sent it over, free of charge.

This amount covered half the Monastery. A woman who noticed we had not finished painting explained that her uncle was in the paint business and if Mother didn't mind, she would ask him for the rest. He sent just enough to finish the other side of the building with a pint left over.

As the walls were going up, Bishop Toolen arrived unexpectedly one day and was surprised that the building was so large. At the time, Mother was asking to borrow money from the bank to finish and needed his approval. Bishop Toolen's solution was to let half the building go unfinished and have the sisters sleep in the workroom area until the money could be found to finish. This would have meant leaving all the steel bar-joices exposed to rust and closing the chapel before this side was finished. It would have meant that the concrete floor could never be poured. Mother was distraught. When the bishop left she went out to tell the workmen. They became so upset, they told her, "Don't worry, Mother, you don't have to pay us till you have the money. We will go ahead and finish the building. Pay us when you can." God rewarded their generosity by giving us enough donations to pay all we owed.

From the time we put up the original Monastery until this day, all the block, mortar, sand and concrete have been donated by the De Marco family—father, and then son.

Founding sisters: (back row) Sister Joseph, Sister Raphael, Sister Assumpta, Sister Michael, (seated) Mother Angelica

CHAPTER FIVE

Bound for Alabama

On May 8, 1962, the day finally arrived when Mother Angelica returned to Canton to take the sisters she had chosen for the new foundation to Alabama and begin a new phase of our religious life.

With mixed emotions, we prepared to leave the Monastery where I had spent eleven years and Mother fifteen. At that time, because the Vatican Council had not made its proclamations bringing cloistered life into the 20th century, we assumed that we would never see these beautiful sisters again. We had shared many joys and sorrows together and knew we were beginning an adventure without them. Our parents, too, were there to say goodbye and watched us drive away, wondering if they too would ever be able to make the trip to Alabama.

A friend had offered his station wagon for the trip and we drove for two days to reach our destination. Mother Angelica, her mother, Sisters M. Joseph, Michael, Assumpta, and myself, were to be followed in August by Mother M. Veronica.

A week before dedication a man named Joe Bruno, who had a chain of supermarkets, came through the Monastery.

He was very touched by Mother's description of our monastic life and by the purpose of having sisters in adoration before the Blessed Sacrament, praying for the people of the world. When the tour was complete, he told her he would donate all our food for an entire year. She was overwhelmed. She had not even thought of the expense involved in feeding five sisters.

When the year was out and she called to thank Joe for the generosity he replied, "Mother, as long as I have a supermarket, you and your sisters will have food." When we came to Birmingham, Joe had thirteen supermarkets. Now twenty years later, he has fifty-six, and fifty drug stores. Last year someone asked him if he was still feeding the sisters and he replied, "I can't afford not to!"

On May 20, 1962, we closed the cloister doors and the Chapel was dedicated for perpetual adoration and called Our Lady of the Angels. A dream had come true. We had a monastery, but as the bills began to come in we realized we also had a $90,000 debt. It took five years, but through the generosity of the people of Birmingham, who cared about us and the Lord, we were able to pay it off.

LEARNING ABOUT HOLINESS

We had a lesson by Mother Angelica every morning after breakfast so she could teach us her ideals for our community. Her only thought was that each of us would become holy. "Show me one saint that imitated another saint to become holy," she declared. "You can't, because you can't be somebody else and become a saint. You must be yourself imitating Jesus.

"You never read that Jesus remade His apostles. He never sat down and told them, 'Now Peter, you're impulsive and blustering. You must become someone else.' No. Our Divine Lord used what he found in their individual natures and worked from there—grace building on nature.

"It's easy to talk about the family spirit and treating each sister as a mature individual, but we must learn to do it; to respect the opinions and ideas of others even when they do not correspond with our own. We must realize the tremendous importance of each sister, chosen by God as a spouse of Christ and carrying Jesus in her soul. What we do to each one, we are really doing to Jesus. After all, He created these souls and gave them their individuality. We can't expect to have contact with Him in prayer when our attitude toward Him in our neighbor all day is wrong. By refusing to love one person, we build up a wall around ourselves. Then we criticize others because they sense it and withdraw from us. We are the only one who can take down the wall."

Mother made every effort to instill the Franciscan spirit into the community. "You can always have joy—it doesn't depend on pleasure. That's the mistake people make. They think if they don't find pleasure in everything, they can't be happy. Real joy is never affected by pain or hardship. It rejoices in God's Will and accepts everything from God's Hands and then there is always happiness.

"Joy should be the mark of a Franciscan. Everything that happens should be new and beautiful and we should realize that it came from God's Hands—this sunrise, the gifts people bring, the rain, the mail." We determined that every gift brought to the Monastery would first be put on the altar for Jesus to see.

Mother enjoyed relating examples of the saints whose uniqueness caused them difficulties.

"In order for a person to be canonized, there must be proof of joy in their lives. John Bosco was persecuted because he was taking young ruffians off the streets of Italy and teaching them trades and how to be holy. The government thought he was gathering an army of rebels while some of the churchmen felt guilty and jealous for not equaling him in zeal.

"Two priests decided that he was not holy, but crazy, and so they devised a plot to trap him into going for a ride with them, not as a pleasure trip, but to take him to the nearest insane asylum.

"John Bosco, however, was warned of their intentions. As the two conspirators urged him into the carriage, he suddenly 'remembered' his manners and as a simple priest, stepped back politely to allow them to enter the carriage ahead of him. As the two stepped in, he slammed the door and called excitedly to the driver, 'Off to the asylum!' The two had a difficult time proving they were not the sick ones.

"Philip Neri was such a clown the young men crowded into his apartment at night and carried on with great joy. To the complaints of the other priests who wanted to sleep he said, 'I don't care if they chop fire wood on my back as long as they do not offend God!'

"Great St. Teresa once complained to Our Lord, 'Your Majesty, if I had my way, that woman would not be Superior.' And Jesus replied, 'Daughter, if I had My way, she wouldn't be either.' So you see, Jesus doesn't always have His way. He allows things to happen to keep from hampering our free will."

CHAPTER SIX

Changes

In an area with only 2% Catholic population, we realized that our veiled faces and grilled parlors were rather forbidding. About two years after dedication, when the pronouncements of Pope John XXIII's Second Vatican Council were circulated, we revised our Rules to allow for more practical living of the enclosure and petitioned Rome for the necessary Indult (permission).

By this time the fishing lures had been abandoned. "Southern fish wouldn't bite on Yankee lures," quipped Mother Angelica. A common way for monasteries to support themselves is by making altar breads for the nearby churches. Since the diocese already had a source, we decided to replace this means of maintaining our Monastery and began to roast peanuts to sell to concessions. We bought the necessary equipment and turned two of the workrooms into roasting, cooling and packaging rooms. We bought a van and hired a salesman to sell the bags to local supermarkets and we shipped them out of town to concession stands at racetracks and football stadiums. This business lasted about two years until we were asked for a kickback from a buyer. Mother stated flatly that we were not going to lose our souls over peanuts. We sold the equipment and decided from then on we would live on Divine Providence and to this day He has provided for us in every way.

Around 1970, we built fountains on the rocks in front of the Monastery. We donned straw hats and aprons and cut all the pine trees that were growing in the crevices—swept loose sand and carried rocks off the surface to prepare for the necessary pipes to be laid. Water was piped from our well into a walled area to collect and be recycled over the rocks. It was a glorious sight. A grotto of water gushed up around a statue of Our Lady of the Angels. A local church was redecorating and gave us four beautiful carrara marble angels. These were placed on either side of Our Lady's statue facing the Chapel. Around this setting, we arranged groups of flowering plants.

Each day as we were out working on the hot rocks, a priest would drive up in his air conditioned car and ask Mother to let him pray over her for the baptism of the Holy Spirit. "I received the Holy Spirit when I was baptized, Father," she said and thought to herself, "get lost." Day after day he would come, make his request and then proceed to make a holy hour in the air conditioned chapel while we were working on the rocks. "Many thoughts went through my mind," Mother related before an audience at St. Leo's Abbey in Florida. "Some of them I can't repeat here. Finally, in desperation I said, 'OK, Father, what do you want me to do?'" He indicated that he wanted her to sit in a chair while he prayed over her. "Is that it?" she asked when he was finished.

"That's it," he replied.

"If I'd known that's all you wanted, I'd have gotten rid of you long ago." Father laughed slyly and went away.

About a week later she came down with a summer cold. "I always enjoy poor health," she continued her story. "I like to sit in bed eating bonbons and reading the mortified lives of the saints. My sisters are very germ-conscious and they wear surgical masks and hand me juice at arm's length.

"As I sat there with my Bible, I decided to read the Gospel of St. John out loud. 'In the beginning was the Word and the Word was with God and the Word was God...' Suddenly a new experience of the Spirit came upon me. Sister Regina came in with some orange juice and I made a sign that I couldn't talk. Then, I left my room and my cold was gone. Afterwards, I went out in front of the fountains, walking back and forth for some time."

It was two months before she shared the experience with the community. The week before Easter, she began praying over the sisters and one by one we each began a new relationship with the Spirit.

Charismatic groups were springing up around the country and questions were being asked by concerned Catholics who saw their loved ones leaving the Church and joining other denominations. Mother could see how the excitement of the new experience and charisma could be misleading to lay people, due to the danger of emotionalism and lack of adherence to the Sacraments and in-depth spirituality. When different groups called to ask her for teachings, she gave her time freely and generously to help them get back on solid ground and doctrine. They needed deep Catholic spirituality to grow in holiness. Knowledge of the ways of God in the soul and the necessity of the Sacraments were essential. Instead of letting them leave the Church, she showed them how the grace of the Sacraments was essential.

It was at this time Mother was invited to a meeting for the purpose of discussing the needs of the diocese. She realized that to help the people grow spiritually, they needed to be taught how to pray. As her contribution, she wrote a format for prayer and called it *Journey into Prayer.* Mother presented new insights on Scripture that helped lay people in their daily lives.

We were all excited as we helped Mother find Scripture passages from the Old Testament to bring out the tenderness of the Heavenly Father's Love. We got folders and made copies for each member of the committee and when the meeting was called, Mother presented her book to them for discussion. However, they had already decided that parish visits and committee meetings were what they wanted for the diocese and the book was put aside as a possible third phase. They did not share her vision.

Mother was crushed. She came home stunned and unbelieving. There had been no purpose to the book at all.

CHAPTER SEVEN

The Book Apostolate

The sisters were all convinced that the booklet was inspired and would be fruitful for souls, so with the Bishop's approval and an imprimatur (a declaration that there is no wrong doctrine in the book) from St. Bernard's monks in Cullman, we had it printed in a local shop. We obtained a copyright under the title *Journey into Scripture 1973.* Included in the copyright were the cassette tapes we were producing. Mother was speaking to an interdenominational group of women who were meeting once a week. By the time the talks were discontinued, there were 250 talks on a great variety of subjects.

This first book was followed by another, concerning theological values. We talked it over at table and decided to name it *In the Shadow of His Light.*

Each book, as it was forming in Mother's mind, was written in her yellow tablet and read to the community at lesson, where we discussed it and asked questions. Mother related to a reporter one day, "The sentences seem to form, I see them and write them down. When the light turns out in my mind, I know the book is finished." No book is ever edited. I would take the manuscript after Sister Veronica had typed and checked it for spelling and punctuation. Three of us would go over the proofs that came back from the printer. I would design a cover subject to the community's approval and we would have the book printed.

A friend hit on the idea of taking twelve pages of excerpts from the large books and calling them "Mini-books." One printed sheet of paper made a twelve page booklet after it was folded and stapled. We began to give them away to people traveling through Birmingham. Soon we were receiving requests from all over the world. Seeing the potential in the smaller books, Mother concentrated on writing these smaller books.

By this time the books had been given out free and were being spread everywhere. We were receiving orders for them through the mail. Some people gave donations, others did not, but all received the books they requested. Anyone who came to visit the Monastery was given a box of books to distribute when he left. We ask people to drop the books like seeds and let God bring the increase. Glowing reports came to us of people being converted by finding a book in a hotel room or phone booth. Several had found a book as they were on their way to commit suicide and their lives were so changed they determined to start over.

When we had printed about seventeen books, our printer announced that the firm was no longer doing this kind of work. Knowing we could not afford another printer's prices, Mother brought the problem before the community for discussion. "Unless we print the books ourselves," she said, "we will not be able to have them anymore." We decided to buy one press and print the books at the Monastery.

Everyone Mother talked to discouraged her. "What will you do when the machinery breaks down?" friends would ask. They couldn't see nuns with ink on their hands.

Sister Regina and Mother went over to the printing company showroom to buy a press. Mother had one of the large books under her arm and when the salesman asked what she wanted to print she showed it to him.

"What are you printing with now?" the salesman wanted to know. Mother explained that she did not have a press, nor did she know how to print. "But this book is four color work," he observed and began looking around for the manager. Mother repeated her story to him and by this time was getting exasperated.

"Do you want to sell me a press or not?" she asked.

"Yes, Mother, but how will you learn to run it?"

"If it takes more than twenty minutes, you can forget it," she said. Then noticing a press on the floor, she told him she thought she could run that one. It had a button, a switch and two gadgets! He told her it cost $9,000. "I'll take it," she told him. Of course he didn't know she had only $200.

When she said she'd take it, she could see Sister Regina sitting on a stool and beginning to slump lower and lower. By the time she picked out a cutter and stapler, she had spent $13,000.

"Do you know what you just did?" Regina asked incredulously as they left. "Where will you get the money?"

"At a bank," Mother announced triumphantly. "They have plenty of it and we need some."

Well, they went from bank to bank and no one would give them a loan. "Why won't you give us a loan?" Mother finally asked impatiently.

"You have no collateral, Mother," explained the banker.

"I have a monastery that's paid for."

"Mother," he answered and by this time he had lowered his voice condescendingly, "I can't take the Monastery for collateral. If you default, this city would kill us! Mother, what are your assets?"

"If I had any I wouldn't be here!" Mother exclaimed.

"Mother," he tried again, "what is your monthly income?"

"I won't know till the end of the month," she replied.

"Mother," he pleaded desperately, "are you asking me to give you a loan on faith? Do you expect me to go to the Board of Directors of this bank and say I gave Mother Angelica $13,000 on faith?"

"Yes," she assured him.

"I can't do that!" he protested.

"Pagan!" she exclaimed. "And he was a Christian pagan too!"

About a week before the equipment was to be delivered, we still did not have the money. A friend came by to chat one morning and jokingly Mother hit him on the shoulder and said, "How would you like to lend me $10,000?"

"OK," he answered.

"Are you joking?" she asked in surprise.

"No, are you?" he questioned.

"I was, but I'm not now."

That afternoon, he returned with a check for $10,000 and in three months Our Lord had paid him back.

Mother was never one to do things by halves. She determined to do the whole operation at the Monastery and not have to go outside for negatives or typesetting the copy.

Over the protests of all of us, she ordered a camera for $4,500. It wasn't the cost we objected to but the fact that we knew it took brains to enlarge and reduce art work and none of us felt qualified. Since she had me in mind to operate it, she ordered one that was most simple to use.

Unknown to her, a huge sink was to come with the camera and one morning it arrived. The man who knocked at the door was livid as he angrily exclaimed, "Did anyone think of measuring the doorway before they ordered the sink?" Mother took a look at the sink and began to get weak in the knees. It was indeed the largest sink she had ever seen.

"Why don't we try it?" she asked.

"This sink will not fit through that door!" he exclaimed, punctuating each word as he spoke. Even our inexperienced eyes could see he was right.

"Well, let's pray over it," Mother insisted doggedly.

"God Almighty can't get this sink through that door. It took three men to put it on the truck and now you want us to take it off just to prove it won't go through the door?"

"Try it," she said as convincingly as she could. "I'll pray."

Seeing there was no way to dissuade her, the three men huffed and puffed and struggled with the sink and they had an inch to spare! We never knew whether the Lord shrunk the sink or widened the door!

A few days later before the camera was to be delivered, we were visited by some dear friends from out of town and they wanted to know what was happening. Mother told them about the camera and the story of the sink. They wanted to know how much the camera and sink had cost. Before they left, they had decided that the wife's birthday present would be our new camera and they wrote out a check.

One day Mother had a novel idea: to make a little book half the size of a Mini-book. One would be for children and one a capsulized presentation of the faith. She called the man who had sold her the other equipment.

"Charlie, have you got a slitter?" she asked.

"Yes, Mother," he replied.

"Will it cut a Mini-book in two?"

"It will if you say so, Mother," he promised.

When the machine arrived, the same man who had brought the sink, brought the slitter. Mother noticed as she approached him that he was upset again.

"You bought a pig in a poke!" he shouted. "Why didn't you ask me before you ordered this thing?"

"What's the matter?" Mother asked.

"There's no way this book will go through that machine. You see, the roller is here (to the left of the book) and the other is here (to the right of the book) and the book is here (to the center)!"

"Let's try it," Mother said with a show of enthusiasm. She could see herself that it looked impossible.

"Mother, God Almighty can't put this book through that slitter!" he repeated.

"Let's pray over it." Mother was trying to calm him.

"You pray over it," he was triumphant now as he waited for her to prove he was right.

Mother picked up a pack of books and, with pretended confidence and a prayer in her heart, put them into the machine and pulled down the roller to lock them in. When she snapped the switch they began shooting out in pairs like bullets out of a machine gun.

Amazed, he asked, "How did you do that?"

Mother responded, "I don't know, let's sneak up on it."

He leaned over the machine in mystified silence.

It happened that as the books dropped into the machine, each pushed the next one against the blade and through the slitter.

He told us later that he had called the plant in Michigan about some other equipment and casually remarked to the service man there that the nuns were slitting a book 3" x 6" in size. "It can't be done," came the crisp reply.

"Don't tell me what they can't do, I'm telling you what they're doing!"

And so we accumulated the necessary machinery to finish the books. The guiding policy was to buy the best kind of equipment that would do the greatest amount of work in the shortest amount of time. We worked four and a half hours a day and were careful not to disrupt our monastic life. Times set aside by our rule for prayer and recreation were carefully adhered to so that the work, however worthy, did not infringe on our contemplative life. We knew we needed to be spiritually fed so the work would be the fruit of our union with God.

As the book ministry grew and the demand for free books increased, we bought enough equipment to do the work. We soon had four presses which Sister Emmanuel was able to run at one time. Printers often came over to see her writing a letter while the presses clanged and whirred around her. Their mouths would drop open in wonder as they came in the door.

We had two large binding and stapling machines and a heavy duty folder, plus a typesetting machine. By this time, a room had to be added to the Monastery to accommodate the growing apostolate. With only two hundred dollars, we started the building and each week enough contributions for the booklets would come in the mail so that we were always able to pay the workmen. When the room was finished, we placed this sign over the door: "WE DON'T KNOW WHAT WE'RE DOING, BUT WE'RE GETTING GOOD AT IT!"

EUCHARISTIC CONGRESS

A school teacher in New Jersey was quick to see the good being done by the booklets when she began to read them to her 4th and 5th graders. She took advantage of the booklets on the sacraments by teaching them in her classroom. After school when the youngsters went home with her, she taught them about prayer and the Scriptures. In this way, a prayer group of children began. She told us by phone that they simply loved the messages and did not want to go home for supper. Some of them shared peanut butter sandwiches with her and stayed till their parents came for them.

As the year for the Eucharistic Congress approached and the teacher learned it would be held in Philadelphia, she called and asked if we could supply enough books to have a booth. She offered to stay at the booth with some of the children and hand out Mini-books. Mother had already sent in the fee for a booth and was granted first choice of places, which turned out to be the booth immediately in front of the escalator where everyone had to enter the hall.

The children were excited. Trained by their excellent teacher to approach bishops and monsignori and to address them properly, they prepared for the Congress with great zeal.

The Eucharistic Congress was of special interest to us since our lives are dedicated to the Eucharist and perpetual adoration. The Congresses are held all over the world and the Blessed Sacrament (Eucharist) is venerated in magnificent ways with pageantry and ceremony by the highest dignitaries of the Church. Processions and teachings are held for a week and religious orders display vocational and occupational material in booths for members of the Church to see.

I was busy making enlargements of book covers, painting and decorating the finished pictures with bright colored poster boards to decorate the booth. Vera, the grade school teacher made plans also for decorating and urged the children to use their own ideas.

Pope Paul IV's Encyclical (letter) on evangelism stated that NOW was the time to evangelize and that it was the duty of every man, woman and child in the Church. We were encouraged by his words and began to pack and ship the booklets for the Congress. Box after box was sent to New Jersey and the children made packets in envelopes that we had specially designed and printed. They were to be presented to the people who came to the Congress.

When the day arrived, two of the children stationed themselves at the escalator and directed people to our booth where a slide program had been prepared by a businessman who came to the Monastery and took the necessary photographs of the apostolate.

Once the Congress was in progress, Vera realized that she was quickly running out of booklets due to the great zeal of the six children. They would not even stop for lunch and had obtained permission from their parents to stay till ten o'clock every evening.

One young boy approached a bishop. He pushed his way through the crowd and pressed the sample of booklets into his hands, asking if he had heard of Mother Angelica. The latter was so delighted with the youngster's enthusiasm, that he allowed himself to be led to the booth where he watched the slide program and talked with Vera.

Meanwhile, back at the Monastery, we were packing more books and taking boxes to the airport to send air freight so they would arrive before the Congress was over. For four days the children distributed booklets.

At the Congress, another child wanted to give books to a rather serious looking bishop, who replied that he did not have time to stop. The young boy exclaimed, "Aw, Bishop, don't be such a grouch!" The bishop's face lit up with a smile and he walked over to the booth with Timmy to see the display.

As well as we could figure, we had shipped and they had distributed 150,000 Mini-books and leaflets!

Within two years the press room would not hold all the equipment and packing necessary to fill the influx of orders. So we added what we came to call the Miracle Room. In two months time, God provided the workers and material to erect a room 35 x 72 ft.

CHAPTER EIGHT

Doing the Ridiculous

"Unless we are willing to do the ridiculous,
God will not do the miraculous."

This is Mother's favorite motto when referring to the apostolate. She explains: "Once I know God is evolving events in such a way that His Will is evident, I jump in. I'm afraid the time will pass and I'll miss the opportunity." This sentence epitomizes Mother Angelica's motivation. This is the woman I have admired, loved and followed for thirty years. She is holy, full of the Holy Spirit, fiercely loyal to the Church and very much in love with God.

"So often we toss our ideas to a committee we have in our head, and begin to talk ourselves out of everything by reasoning," she explained to us at lesson one morning. "The process of doing God's Will is simple. First I see the purpose of the action, to promote the Church and further the Kingdom. An inspiration suggests a way to achieve this. I begin the process immediately. If the Lord keeps evolving it, I push on and look for the fruit, taking the risk of failure. I would rather fail by trying.

The greatest failure to me is not trying at all."

We got involved in television like we have with everything else, with a simple inspiration. Mother explains: "We had been invited to Chicago to Channel 38 in March of 1978 for an interview. It was just a tiny station on top of a large building and as soon as I walked in there I said, 'Lord, I gotta have one of these!' Of course it did cross my mind—what would twelve cloistered nuns do with a television studio, but I put the thought quickly aside, because I knew it was one great way to stifle the Spirit."

As they drove away, Mother said to the friend who was driving, "Tom, I gotta have one of these!"

"What, Mother?" he asked.

"A television station or studio or something!"

Sister Joseph was sitting in the back seat praying and the Lord said to her, "Tell Mother the media is Mine and I give it to her."

"Are you joking?" Mother asked.

"I don't think He was," Sister replied.

Mother has a knack for simplifying things and getting to the heart of the matter. "Isn't it wonderful when you don't know what you're doing and you just begin? You see we have succumbed to corporation methods. We have to have everything pat, all the money we need, all the talent, all the capability and then with some absolute guarantee of success, we begin. By that time, we forget what we started to do."

When she got home, Mother questioned Jean Morris, who had been in Chicago with her as traveling companion. Jean is an Episcopalian who had become a friend of ours during the time Mother was giving weekly talks to interdenominational groups at the Monastery several years prior to this.

"Where do we go to make a television tape?" Mother asked.

Jean didn't know but promised to find out. She found this little studio, a hole-in-the-wall operation, and the three of us went over to see what would happen.

The studio was different for Mother. In Chicago, there had been an audience to respond to but here, there was nothing but a camera with legs behind it.

Mother wanted to call the series *Our Hermitage* and build a monastic setting with a rocking chair, a candle, a bench and two or three books, "to make me look intelligent," Mother said later. The format would be simple. She would walk in, light the candle, stand behind the rocking chair and greet the people. She would then come around in front and sit in the rocking chair. After a twenty minute message, she would get up, go behind the chair and blow out the candle.

As she came on the set, the microphone cord was dangling at her side since it was pinned to her collar and she kept brushing it behind her as she walked in. Leaning over to light the candle, she was surprised to hear someone shout, "CUT!"

"What's the matter?" she wanted to know.

"You just popped off the screen," complained the director, "start again."

They decided to omit the candle lighting and go on. Later, Mother described the results to a delighted crowd of people in Michigan.

"There I was, walking on like a baby elephant, pushing the mic cord behind me. I sat down looking like Grandma Moses, with an Andy Gump profile and a Mickey Mouse voice. Finally I leaned over and blew out the unlit candle."

As we rode home that afternoon, there was silence in the car. Mother finally announced, "Why don't we just admit that I don't have it and quit?"

Jean and I were emphatic. "You do have it and we're going back until we bring it out of you."

We designed a new set that was warm and homey and after several attempts, came up with a complete half-hour program on a small tape that cost us $1,000.

This tape was too precious to put in the mail so Mother asked Jean to fly up to Portsmouth, Va. and present it to someone at the Christian Broadcasting Company for an audition. When Jean arrived at CBN however, she learned her appointment had been cancelled. Jean explained why she had come and finally was directed to the program manager. He was amazed to hear her story. Later he told Mother the staff had been praying to find a Catholic program for the Network. He told Jean he would listen to the tape and call us.

In two weeks, Mother received a call from him saying CBN would be proud to use our program. Would she be able to make sixty? Mother was so elated and flabbergasted she said yes without realizing it meant $60,000 at the going rate. She called Jean and when we finally came down from the clouds, we decided to scout around for a less expensive place to make the tapes. By taking our sets to a local station and buying our tapes in bulk, we could pay for three hours of time and make as many programs as possible.

Jean and I designed the set and had it constructed. She made appointments to go to the studio twice a week. We would load her car with flower arrangements and knickknacks to put on the fireplace and haul everything to the studio at the station. The crew would be waiting to set up and by one o'clock we would start. Jean would apply Mother's makeup. I would be sure the cameras were picking up her best angles. We would all say a prayer with the cameramen and director and Mother would open the Scriptures. The floorman would count down from ten after rolling the *Our Hermitage* opening we had made. Then and only then did God give Mother the words to say. Her mind was a total blank until the countdown was ended. She would speak for twenty-eight minutes and take a five minute break. I would run from my place in the control room, get the title of the next program from her, give her a glass of water and we would make another tape. Every afternoon we would come home with four quad tapes and four three-quarter tapes of the four half-hour programs we had done. Before we would leave, the crew would gather around Mother to ask her questions about the program content. As the weeks went by, the crew became impressed with Mother's sincerity and deep conviction.

After we had made the sixty programs called *Our Hermitage* which were on the Gospels, we became more adventurous and decided on another series to explain the Epistles. We called it *In His Sandals.*

Mother, Jean and I went to look for a mural of a landscape to put outside a large bay window which we could use on the new set. Finding an autumn scene, we brought it home and with the help of several sisters, pasted it to the two large 4' x 8' prop boards. We painted two other boards to look like cream colored paneling and arranged them to form a corner of a room. A chair, table, lamp and plants were added and we were ready to start.

We were on our seventeenth segment of *In His Sandals* the day we learned of a blasphemous movie to be aired in the very station at which we were producing. The synopsis of the plot for this movie, called *The Word,* described the finding of an ancient scroll that proved Jesus was not God, did not die on the cross and that the Resurrection was a hoax.

After our taping session, we made an appointment with the manager of the station. Mother described the damage that would be done in the minds of viewers who would be influenced by the bad seed sown by this blasphemy. She stated that since he admitted to being a Christian, he would not want to promote anything so offensive to God.

"Do you think God cares what we do down here?" he asked.

"Yes, He cares," Mother affirmed, "and I care."

"Are you telling me what kind of programs to put on my station?" he asked.

"Me? Tell you what to put on your station? I think you have crummy programs on your station. I've been coming here three months and I haven't said a word to you about your crummy programs." Mother kept her cool, but it wasn't easy.

"Well, I intend to show the movie," he answered with determination.

"That's your decision?" she asked. "Then I intend to make one. I will not sign this contract to air my programs on your station, and I will not make any more programs in your studio. It's against my principles to condone blasphemy!"

"You can't do that," he exclaimed. "You leave here and you're off television. There's not another studio within a hundred miles of here. You need us."

"No, I don't need you," she countered, "I only need God. I'll buy my own cameras and build my own studio."

"You can't do that," he said in disbelief.

"You just watch me!" she replied.

By that time, we were all standing and leaving the office. Out in the hall, the air was strangely still and no one was in sight. The usually busy corridors were empty.

When we arrived home the sisters were all anxious to hear what had happened. "I blew it," Mother told them, "I told him I would build my own studio, but I wouldn't know where to start."

"The garage!" everybody cried in unison. "We'll turn it into a studio."

We trooped downstairs behind the Monastery. There had been fifteen hundred blocks left over after building the packing room and we were about to build a garage for the car and tractor. Mother instructed the yardman to dig the footer longer and wider.

That was the beginning of the Eternal Word Television

Network. Since Mother had started it in defense of The Word, we all felt it to be an appropriate title. It was November 1, 1978.

The next day, we went back to the studio to load two pick-up trucks with the sets and props we had been using. The crew gathered around in surprise and concern. "You're not going through with this, are you? Wait till the movie is over and then come back."

"No," Mother told them, "we cannot act as though nothing happened. It's time somebody took a stand against the filth that is presented on television."

The news began to spread and the editor of the religious page of the local newspaper came to get the story. Before the movie was ever shown, a story appeared to warn people of the danger to their souls in watching a blasphemous movie. Not one other voice was raised against it; not one other program was cancelled at that studio. We stood alone in defense of the Eternal Word.

A few days later a friend called from Florida to catch up on the news and was filled in on the latest happening. As the realization of what it meant to have a Catholic network began to dawn on Mother, she explained it to her Florida caller.

"Good for you!" Lee exclaimed with enthusiasm. "It's time somebody stood up for something. Television gets worse and worse. I'm going to help you, Mother. I'll write to all the prayer groups in Florida and tell them what happened. We're going to build that studio."

As the walls began to rise on the Eternal Word Studio, the people of Florida responded. Every week as we needed money to pay bricklayers and workmen, the checks came in with encouraging words from the people who had caught the vision. We never had more than we needed, always just enough and just in time.

"Just in time" is becoming a motto at the Monastery. Jesus

never gives us more than we need. He always demands faith from week to week. As we have discussed many times at lesson in the morning, when an opportunity comes to do something for God and we have agreed that it is His apparent Will, the opportunity, had we not acted, would have passed. The people, circumstances and times would have changed so much that another period of time would have made it impossible. The opportunity, if not taken, would have been gone forever.

We knew that many of our friends did not feel the studio was a reasonable or practical thing to build. Some admitted later that they thought it was an ego trip. But the urging of the Holy Spirit within our community was unmistakable and it is better to appear foolish before men than to answer to God for being afraid to step out and trust Him. After all the miracles He has worked here, we feared that, like Moses, we might be tempted to strike the rock twice and bring down His anger.

It is better to fail than to disappoint the Father. Faith has never been an easy virtue for Mother Angelica to practice. She has often described her struggles to us.

"The first time the inspiration came to me about building a television studio and network, it was followed by the thought, 'What would twelve cloistered nuns do with a satellite dish in their back yard?' I immediately brushed that aside because it's the quickest way to stifle the Spirit. I began to watch God evolve the situation and as a door opened, I stepped through, even though reason rebelled at the risk and the debt that had to be assumed. I was shaking inside and scared to death the first time I ordered television equipment. As the cost loomed before me and I saw the impossibility of being able to pay by any human standards, I was overwhelmed by the responsibility involved. I can't tell you how many times I had my hand on the telephone to call and cancel the order but each time something would happen to call me away from it. Some big company would be willing to give credit with no more collateral than my signature, or there would be an opportunity to borrow at low interest."

"Faith, to me, is one foot in the air, one on the ground, and a queasy feeling in your stomach. I take a lot of Maalox. Someone said to me, 'Mother, you are a woman of such great faith, why do you take Maalox?' I told her, 'Because my stomach doesn't know I have faith.'"

When our studio was complete, we made a trip to a studio in Atlanta to make some programs and look at an infinity wall. This wall can be used for special effects and projected pictures can be made to look like actual scenery behind the speaker. We came home and described the wall to our contractor. Since he knew something about building boats, he was sure he could make the floor sweep up into the wall to look like infinity. When he got it completed, we painted it gray according to the formula and behold, there it was, infinity at one end and a black limbo wall at the other.

It was time to order quartz lights to hang from the ceiling of the studio. A salesman from New York came to determine what we would need. After looking over the studio he told Mother that $48,000 would buy all the essential lighting. "Go back and sharpen your pencil," Mother told him, "there's no way we can pay that much for lights." Slightly stunned, the man listened to her tell the dream of having the Church on television and what it would mean for the spiritual growth of the people. He began to catch the vision and went outside to go over his figures again. Finally he returned.

"The best I can do is $14,800."

"Sold!" exclaimed Mother and she hurried inside to tell us that we were getting the best kind of lights for $30,000 less than the original price.

A few weeks later, Frank, the light salesman, called from New York. "Mother," he began, "when I came down in the price from $48,000 to $14,000 you didn't think you would be getting the same lights, did you?"

"Of course I did," Mother answered. "I want the very best for Our Lord."

"Well," he proceeded, "let me tell you what happened. The lights are made in Italy. When I called in the order they told me that because cheaper lights would take six weeks to ship, they were sending the expensive kind, but that I should only charge you the lower price."

Someone asked Mother what would have happened if she failed with this project. "Well," she replied, "I guess I'd have the most lit up garage in the world!"

Mother had decided to step out in faith and order the most needed items of equipment, a camera and one recorder, to get started. She had been assured it would be six weeks before they arrived and would have to be paid for, but a week later a man arrived from Texas with the camera. She was shocked to think that this man expected $24,000. As she went in to shake hands with him she said. "I hope you know the good news, I don't have the money to pay for this?"

He took her hand with a smile and said, "Yes, isn't it thrilling!"

Mother was about to leave for a conference in Michigan and from there travel on to Ohio for a four day speaking engagement. As she addressed the people of Muskegon, she told them her dream of having a satellite dish in her back yard beaming beautiful spirituality all over the country. She told the story of the lights and camera. The people gave her a standing ovation when they heard that their children would be having sound doctrine taught to them through animated Scripture. A collection was taken and they gave her the unbelievable offering of $20,000. By the time she completed the tour, she had enough to pay for the camera. While she was there, a camper van had been parked outside the stadium so she could rest in it between talks. It gave her an idea. "Lord, I gotta have one of these!" she prayed.

With a mobile unit to carry the television equipment while she was on the road, talks could be taped and a library accumulated of speakers who could teach on the Network. The Muskegon prayer group had a van custom-made and took up the payments on it. When it was completed, three of the men drove it to Birmingham.

By this time, we had ninety half-hour programs which we were sending around the country to cable stations and for closed-circuit in hospitals and prisons. They have become permanent library material in one hundred and twenty prisons in this country.

Mother began receiving invitations to speak at large conferences. People were finding her approach to holiness not only delightfully humorous, but practical and imitable. She has a gift for finding out where people are and bringing them closer to God.

"I want everything done yesterday!" she exclaimed to a group. "There's no Italian born patient!" The crowd identified with her and leaned forward to hear more.

She has a rare charisma. She is recognized as holy, but also human. People gather hope for their own souls as they listen to her humorous description for everyday happenings.

Women were writing to her, she told a group at St. Leo's in Florida, complaining that after forty years of marriage, their husbands were leaving them for younger women.

"You men, you see your wife getting gray and wrinkled and you go out looking for some young chick. Let me tell you something. Your bald head is no morning sunrise!"

A staff member of PTL, a Protestant Christian Network, heard Mother speak and invited her to appear in Charlotte, North Carolina and be interviewed by Jim Bakker, the founder of the PTL Network.

It was a day in January 1979, when Jean and I went with her. We sat waiting for her to appear and I was watching the audience as they looked from the live broadcast to the monitors. Mother was called to the floor behind the cameras by the producer, who was telling her not to be nervous, but just go up and answer Jim's questions. As she came on the set, it was obvious that Jim Bakker was not sure how to deal with a real, live Catholic nun. Mother soon put him at ease. In fact, she had him laughing so hard he was almost speechless.

I looked across at the audience. Responding to her sincerity and charm, their attention was sharpened and all were straining to see the live show or pick up the action on the monitors. In rapt attention, they heard her describe the print shop she had built and her efforts to borrow money from the bank to pay for it. Jim was charmed with her wisdom and wit and invited her back. We received many letters from people whose lives were affected by her nitty-gritty approach to holiness.

On one of Mother's return trips to PTL, Jim told her they had taken a poll of the most popular guests and not only had she made the top ten, she was at the top of the top ten. He invited her to co-host the show on one occasion and ran a documentary depicting scenes from the Monastery and studio where he had sent his crew of eleven people to build a set for Mother's first program.

By April 1979, we drew up plans for an addition to the studio and some much-needed office space and began putting together our first documentary.

A crew of five dedicated young people began to take shape. Before long we found ourselves with an engineer, two camera people, a production manager and an audio man.

Mother determined that since the Lord had set the television studio in an atmosphere of prayer, the crew should be drawn into a family setting. She gave lectures each Monday on how to practice virtue and grow together in love and respect. Each morning when they arrived for work, they went in a group to the chapel to begin their day with five minutes of prayer. They met before Jesus in the Blessed Sacrament and had a talk with Him before they worked together. This made the way open for the Holy Spirit to inspire and urge them to be devoted to the work of evangelization through the Network.

On September 18, 1980, Mother ordered the satellite dish and applied for a license from the Federal Communications Commission. Her dream was to reach the common man, teach him the various types of spirituality, provide family programming for children and adults, be a vehicle of expression for various Catholic organizations, to provide inexpensive but high quality programming for dioceses who could not afford to make their own programs.

Through many obstacles and little outside encouragement, Mother has pushed forward to fulfill the inspiration of having a network for the Church where the Holy Father's messages, the Catholic faith and spirituality would be presented in every art form. She has struggled against the opposition of those who should have found means to help her, but instead have set obstacles in her path—obstacles which, but for God's intervention, would have destroyed the Network.

Her desire to feed the people of God has been a constant incentive. She has found them to be hungering for His Word and His truth. She desires to tell the world about Jesus who is present in the Holy Eucharist. Seeing young people come here with no concept of the indwelling of the Trinity in their souls, seeing them risk destroying this temple of the Holy Spirit with drugs and alcohol, makes her realize that the Heart of Jesus is wounded and that she has a moral obligation to spread the truth in every way possible.

It baffles the mind of the learned that twelve cloistered Franciscan nuns could have accomplished what God has done here. The same people who for years have been fond of saying of us, "What do they do all day?" now proclaim in self-defense, "Why don't they stay in their cloister?" The marvel is that we have never left the cloister without proper permissions and sanctions of Rome. Though we stumble and may fail, He will succeed in the work He has inspired and brought to fulfillment.

Mother goes to the mountain like Elias to find her God in prayer. When she hears His Voice in the gentle breeze and senses His gentle urgings, she knows He is near and guiding her. She is not afraid to launch out and fail. Not trying would be to her the greatest failure. Failures teach a lesson no amount of success can impart. She simply goes back to the mountain of prayer and searches for another way to accomplish what she understands to be the Father's Will.

God is a personal God to Mother Angelica as is evidenced by the many books she writes under the guidance of the Holy Spirit. Only He could bring forth the fruits that are attested to by the countless letters that come into the Monastery from those whose lives have been changed.

CHAPTER NINE

The Satellite Dish

"Won't it be funny when people wake up some morning and find that twelve cloistered nuns have a satellite dish in their back yard!" Mother confided to a crowd of 4,000 in Muskegon, Michigan.

Intrigued by the idea, a reporter from *The Wall Street Journal* came the day the dish was to arrive. He spent all day talking to Mother and seeing the dream unfold. Because of rain and mud, the dish was delayed so he did not see it delivered, but he wrote a beautiful article which reached many people who were not aware of our progress.

A call came from *Good Morning America* asking to come and document the first broadcast to go up to the satellite from our station. *Newsweek Video* and the *New York Post* expressed interest. *Twin Circle* sent a reporter from New Orleans to do a story and gave us the four-color cover and an inside center spread, leading off with the caption: "Move over NBC, here comes Mother Angelica!" *PM Magazine* and *People* magazine asked for interviews. Articles began appearing with titles like "The Nuns' Network" and "One Giant Step for Mother Angelica!"

One night during one of our bigger crises, we were praying

in Mother Angelica's bedroom. Sister Regina, in a vision, saw a black sky and the white satellite dish lit up by a flame, coming from the center and going up to heaven. She heard the Heavenly Father say, "This is My Network and it will glorify My Son." It was a consolation to all of us.

A few weeks later the satellite dish arrived. Because the crane was being donated, the men came on Sunday morning to mount the dish on the platform. All of us, along with the crew, crowded around to join in the excitement in our back yard. The day was perfect with blue skies and white clouds. It was high noon.

One of the boys wanted to ride on the crane and was swinging high in the air near the thirty-two foot dish. His brother snapped several pictures of him swinging from the leather belt. When the film was developed and presented to Mother, she became ecstatic. There on the photo was the black sky of the vision with a white dish and a flame coming from the center. John could be seen swinging close to the dish where it had just been hung. No electrical wiring had even been routed to it yet. Excitement ran high in the Monastery. No photographer to whom we have shown the photo has been able to come up with a reasonable explanation. The Heavenly Father had confirmed the vision by an actual photograph.

As pressure and criticism mounted around us, we learned that Cardinal Oddi, head of the Sacred Congregation of Clergy in Rome, was in this country. Bill Steltemeier, President of our Network's Board of Governors, met him in New York and described our television Network and apostolate. The Cardinal agreed to come and see. May 21st, Bill chartered a private plane and he and the Cardinal spent two and a half hours here touring the facilities. His Eminence was delighted and praised Mother Angelica for the work she was accomplishing with twelve nuns and a crew of eleven dedicated people. Cardinal Oddi took Mother by the hand as she led him down the steps to the satellite dish. "This is the only satellite network the Catholic Church has in the world!" he told her. He was elated when she told him of the arrangements being made to tape the Holy Father's Wednesday audience and Sunday Angelus. It was a week since Pope John Paul II had been shot during one of these audiences and we were grateful to have the Cardinal tell us he would see the Pope on the following day and tell him of our progress. Cardinal Oddi described this visit as the highlight of his trip to this country.

After he blessed the satellite dish and transmission room, he came up to the studio and blessed the van and new office buildings. It was a day for celebrations. We presented him with a book of pictures and documents to take back to Rome. He assured us that we would soon have the permissions we needed to carry on the work God was giving our community to do, without changing our status as cloistered nuns.

In our guest book, Cardinal Oddi wrote this beautiful tribute in Italian:

I am happy to bless this initiative which will undoubtedly produce abundant fruits in the field of evangelization.

Since the Lord has permitted human beings to discover some of the secrets of nature, the Church should be the first to utilize the modern methods of transmission.

May the Lord reward most generously this small group of consecrated nuns who have dedicated themselves with such strong faith to the accomplishment of this work.

*~ Silvio Cardinal Oddi Prefect of
the Congregation for the Clergy–21/5/81*

Mother and I made arrangements to attend a cable convention in Los Angeles. We had just received a copy of *Twin*

Circle which carried the full cover picture of Mother with the title "Move Over NBC—Here Comes Mother Angelica." From out of the blue, Mrs. Patrick Frawley, who owned the paper, invited us to stay in her home while we were in Los Angeles.

After landing in Los Angeles, Mother and I drove with Mrs. Frawley to her home near Beverly Hills.

Southern Satellite Systems had offered us a corner of their booth at the Los Angeles Cable Convention for display of our gold brochures.

Mother and I quickly picked up the tempo of the convention and began handing out brochures and talking to cable television people about airing our programs which were on Westar III, transponder 12. The Vice President of SSS began introducing us to people we needed to know and got us invited to the Pioneer Dinner at the Biltmore Hotel where we met all the "founding fathers" of cable television.

When the convention was over, the Frawleys urged us to stay over and meet some people in programming. They invited their good friend and actress Loretta Young to come and help us pick out suitable movies for family viewing.

Loretta arrived and was as lovely and beautiful as I remembered her in her movies. I had never seen any of her television programs as I was in the Monastery by that time, but she expressed the desire for us to have her television movies on the Network. She would see what she could do. As we sat together, I had a chance to tell Loretta about a manuscript of Mother Angelica's life I was working on.

"It would make an interesting movie," I told her, "with the right scriptwriters to handle it. I'm not writing it because I know how to write, but because I feel someone who knows Mother should tell her story."

She was immediately interested. "My producers are coming tomorrow. For seventeen years they have wanted me to come back into television and films." She looked lovingly at Mother Angelica. "I think I could do her life!" she exclaimed. She promised to present the idea the next day and invited us to drop in at her home to join the meeting. With Loretta's declaration that she would only come out of retirement if she could do Mother Angelica's life, plans began to form in that direction and are still in progress as I write. When we arrived home I mailed the first part of my manuscript to Loretta's producer, David Levy.

We were once again faced with the reality of our coming D-Day. August 15th was only two and a half months away. Once we went on the air, we had to have four hours of programs, seven days a week from then on or we were off the air. Mother continued to search for programs that were not only suitable, but also within our price range. Foundation after foundation was saying no to our requests for funding and we were being pushed against the wall.

Things were getting more difficult and we were feeling tremendous pressure. Mother expressed her convictions. "I only know what God is telling me to do. Those who object won't be around when I die and have to face God. I can see God telling other people to support the effort. When they refuse He has to supply the money some other way if He wants this Network."

"Sometimes," she confided to us, "I am so frightened at the burden Our Lord has placed on us. Sometimes my heart is so paralyzed with grief from persecution, that I sit before the Lord numb. I say, 'Lord, I don't see the way, but Your life in me gives me courage for another day.'

"God has put in my heart such a fear of not doing His Will. People ask me how I take so many risks. I feel it's a greater risk to disappoint God. I often think of Moses striking the rock twice and the consequence of his lack of trust. He didn't see the Promised Land."

CHAPTER TEN

We're On the Air!

As August 15, 1981 approached, activity increased along with the excitement. Phones were ringing constantly. Radio stations wanted live telephone interviews. *Good Morning America* wanted a guest appearance; the *Today Show* invited her. Newspapers across the country were doing stories. CNN in Atlanta insisted that she come for an interview. CBS and NBC along with *PM Magazine* had their cameramen here to document the activities. A crew of television cameramen from Germany arrived. They described the tremendous amount of coverage our Network was receiving in their country. They came to do a documentary which would be shown all over Europe. *Voice of America* is sending the story overseas to all English speaking countries. British Television asked to come here and make a program.

All this publicity and we still did not have the money for transponder time. The irony of it all was somehow incredible.

And our crew of beautiful young men and women dedicated to this work were determined not to disappoint Mother or let anyone destroy her dream. For weeks they had been working late into the night to get all the equipment ready and the programs lined up with openings and closings. On the afternoon of August 15th as they sat waiting for the people to begin coming for the procession, Mother went down to express her thanks. As her emotions and gratitude welled up all she could say was, "Thank you!" when a flood of tears began running down her cheeks. Instead of giving a speech, she went from one to another and hugged each one as the men fought back their tears and the women wept openly. It was a day to remember and they had all worked so hard to make it possible.

We had no precedent to follow for the opening of the Network since this had never happened in the Church before. Since we wanted a souvenir to give to everyone, I suggested printing a program and Mother began planning the ceremony.

A procession beginning in the Chapel where the Word was enthroned on the altar began the ceremony. From there a cross bearer and flag bearers led the procession, followed by the nuns of the Monastery, the Board of Governors of the Network, and the crew. Joseph G. Vath, Bishop of Birmingham, and the guests followed. At the door of the control room Mother would read this prayer:

O God, Lord of heaven and earth, You alone have accomplished all we have done. May this first Catholic Satellite Television Network be a tribute to the beauty of Your Church. May Your Son, the Eternal Word, be glorified through this work of Your Hands. Bless all the programs that will issue forth from its facilities. Just as Your Word issues forth from you, Lord Father, may that same Word touch each heart that listens to this Network.

Let Thy Spirit work with freedom through every teacher who proclaims Thy truth and Thy Church.

Bestow upon this Network the power to inspire men to seek holiness of heart, zeal for the extension of Thy Church, cour-

age to seek after justice and human rights and patience to endure persecution.

When the big day arrived everything worked as planned. Mother cut the ribbon outside the control room and went inside to await the moment when she would throw the switch to open the Network—6:00 p.m. August 15, 1981.

We were singing as the moment approached. After a silent prayer, the countdown began—5-4-3-2-1. A cheer went up as Mother threw the switch which sent our first program bouncing off the satellite to homes across America, Canada and part of Mexico. Joy knew no bounds. History was made and we knew the Heart of God was touched.

VOICE
from the
VATICAN

SACRA CONGREGATIO
PRO CLERICIS

Silvio Cardinal Oddi
Prefect of the Congregation for the Clergy

THE ETERNAL WORD TELEVISION NETWORK

April 21, 1982

Have you ever wondered why we usually speak of the Word of God, and not the words of God? Mother Angelica understood the reason very well when she chose the name for The Eternal Word Television Network.

There is, in fact, only one Word of God and it is His Son Our Lord Jesus Christ. "In the beginning was the Word and the Word was with God and the Word was God," we read at the start of the Gospel of St. John. The Eternal Word Network has set as its goal to bring this Word to an audience stretched across the United States of America. There is only one Word, but many tongues are required to make it known, for as the Apostle Paul asked centuries ago: "How can they hear without a preacher?" The Eternal Word Network is, in a sense, one of today's preachers, able to reach far beyond the limited range of a church pulpit into the very homes of individual families .

A year ago I came to Birmingham, Alabama, where the Eternal Word Network has its headquarters, to bless the satellite dish through which the Eternal Word is projected from ocean to ocean. I willingly accepted the invitation to visit because I was of the conviction at that time, and still am, that the Eternal Word Network boasts three characteristics which are of extreme importance in the world of social communications today. These are; fidelity, integrity and modernity.

A faithful preacher of the Word does not preach his or her personal ideas. We are hungry for **God's** Word, not man's. Therefore, the true preacher will find his material not in his own imagination but in what God has communicated to men and women through His revelation and through the sound tradition and teaching of His Church. A reliable preacher will hew strictly to passing on what he has received and will not attempt to invent new teachings. The Church will be his guide in this and conformity with the teaching of the Church is the listener's guarantee that the preacher is preaching the truth.

There is a vast field for individual expression but the core of the message must remain faithful to the Eternal Word. The living tradition of the universal Church must be taken into account when explaining the Scriptures, for God has given men His Church to protect the purity of the transmission of His Word.

I have observed that the Eternal Word Network has taken special pains to listen to the Church and to be guided by the Church in selecting its preachers and teachers and **that** is a source of security and comfort for listeners who tune in to learn what God has to say to them.

The second characteristic of good preaching is integrity. By integrity in this context I do not mean honesty. One takes honesty and sincerity for granted in these matters. By integrity here I mean fullness, completeness. You will recall the old proverb: "a little bit of knowledge is a dangerous thing." Well, that is true in religion, too. A good preacher will give the whole picture and not exaggerate one part of it which he or she happens to prefer. For example, Our Lord said: in Matthew 18: "If your eye causes you to sin, pluck it out and throw it from you." The wise preacher will interpret that vivid literary expression in the light of many other things Our Lord said and did. He will recall how kind Jesus was to the woman taken in adultery, how He cured the lepers, how He promised that His Father would give us **anything** we ask in His name.

Sometimes today's preaching tends to give the impression that true religion consists only of social service. True, Jesus fed the hungry with bread, but He Himself said that not by bread alone does man live. So, balanced, integral preaching will not forget the needs of man's soul, that is, his personal, intimate relationship with the Creator, when it speaks of charity to the materially poor.

21/4/1982 Silvio Card. Oddi
Pref. of J. Conion
for the Clergy

CHAPTER ELEVEN

Cardinal Oddi's Letter

On Cardinal Oddi's trip to Philadelphia in April of 1982, he asked Mother Angelica to meet him on the 22nd and gave her the following statement to publish about his thoughts on the Network.

> *Have you ever wondered why we usually speak of the Word of God, and not the words of God? Mother Angelica understood the reason very well when she chose the name for The Eternal Word Television Network.*
>
> *There is, in fact, only one Word of God and it is His Son Our Lord Jesus Christ. "In the beginning was the Word and the Word was with God and the Word was God," we read at the start of the Gospel of St. John. The Eternal Word Television Network has set as its goal to bring this Word to an audience stretched across the United States of America. There is only one Word, but many tongues are required to make it known, for as the Apostle Paul asked centuries ago: "How can they hear without a preacher?" The Eternal Word Network is, in a sense, one of today's preachers, able to reach*

far beyond the limited range of a church pulpit into the very homes of individual families.

A year ago I came to Birmingham, Alabama, where the Eternal Word Network has its headquarters, to bless the satellite dish through which the Eternal Word is projected from ocean to ocean. I willingly accepted the invitation to visit because I was of the conviction at that time, and still am, that the Eternal Word Network boasts three characteristics which are of extreme importance in the world of social communications today. These are: fidelity, integrity and modernity.

A faithful preacher of the Word does not preach his or her personal ideas. We are hungry for God's Word, not man's. Therefore, the true preacher will find his material not in his own imagination but in what God has communicated to men and women through His revelation and through the sound tradition and teaching of His Church. A reliable preacher will hew strictly to passing on what he has received and will not attempt to invent new teachings. The Church will be his guide in this and conformity with the teaching of the Church is the listener's guarantee that the preacher is preaching the truth.

There is a vast field for individual expression but the core of the message must remain faithful to the Eternal Word. The living tradition of the universal Church must be taken into account when explaining the Scriptures, for God has given men His Church to protect the purity of the transmission of His Word.

I have observed that the Eternal Word Network has taken special pains to listen to the Church and to be guided by the Church in selecting its preachers and teachers and that is a source of security and comfort for listeners who tune in to learn what God has to say to them.

The second characteristic of good preaching is integrity.

By integrity in this context, I do not mean honesty. One takes honesty and sincerity for granted in these matters. By integrity here I mean fullness, completeness. You will recall the old proverb: "a little bit of knowledge is a dangerous thing." Well, that is true in religion, too. A good preacher will give the whole picture and not exaggerate one part of it which he or she happens to prefer. For example, Our Lord said in Matthew 18: "If your eye causes you to sin, pluck it out and throw it from you." The wise preacher will interpret that vivid literary expression in the light of many other things Our Lord said and did. He will recall how kind Jesus was to the woman taken in adultery, how He cured the lepers, how He promised that His Father would give us anything we ask in His name.

Sometimes today's preaching tends to give the impression that true religion consists only of social service. True, Jesus fed the hungry with bread, but He Himself said that not by bread alone does man live. So, balanced, integral preaching will not forget the needs of man's soul, that is, his personal, intimate relationship with the Creator, when it speaks of charity to the materially poor.

It seems to me that the Eternal Word Network has been largely successful in preaching the whole Christ, and not a distorted Christ, a caricature of the Lord. This Network has not set out to prove a personal thesis or to win itching ears to its audience by concentrating on the sensational. On the contrary, it strives to and has been largely successful in presenting Christ and His Church as they truly are, and not as one or another school of theological thought might prefer they should be.

And finally, a good preacher should be contemporary. There are undoubtedly a certain few preachers in history who could be effective in any century. St. Paul is one of these. I think that he would stir up enormous interest even today. On the other hand, styles of transmission of the Word of God do change from age to age and it behooves the Church to keep pace with them because these are the channels for reaching modern man at a given time. Not only do the language, the style, the examples, the literary forms of preaching change from age to age, but even the mechanics, and the Church must keep abreast if she is to reach modern man.

Let me give you an example. It surprised me to find that here in the United States credit cards are sometimes preferred to cash. A customer is sometimes considered more affluent if he flashes a credit card, than if he pays with real money. Whether this is good or bad I do not know, but it seems to be a fact. In a similar way, what people see and hear on television seems often to convince them more immediately than what they might hear in a pulpit on occasions. Television is definitely an important channel into man's mind in our times. Not only does it reach more people and penetrate into the very heart of families where the traditional preaching of the Church could never reach directly, but it possesses a certain internal credibility which could make the Gospel palatable even to people who might otherwise think they had no taste for it. The explanation of this phenomenon is surely arguable, but there is no argument that it is so.

It has been my observation that the Eternal Word Television Network is characterized by this same modernity of which we have been speaking. As a matter of fact, it is in the vanguard of religious communication, certainly in the Catholic Church, by its use of a space satellite to reach its audience. While others have been talking, the Eternal Word has been transmitting. This daring project has begun well. Sensitive to the short interest span of modern men and women, the Eternal Word interlards its more profound messages with healthy entertainment to lighten the heart of man, relax the harried housewife and engross children.

As St. Paul once pointed out to the Athenians, good men and women instinctively worship God, but a God unknown to them by name or person. The Eternal Word Television Network has set out to remove the anonymity from the God Who is surely worshipped in sincerity and truth in millions of families throughout the world. These families will be grateful at last to know Who He is, and what He has said. Anyone who helps this work may also consider himself or herself a faithful, integral, modern communicator of the Eternal Word.

EPILOGUE

A Loyal Friend

Through the early years of the Network, Sr. Raphael continued to joyfully support Mother Angelica's initiatives as her Vicar and friend. In 1987, Our Lady of Angels Monastery celebrated its 25th Anniversary and EWTN began broadcasting 24 hours a day. By 1990, Mother was establishing new production facilities for international shortwave radio, and she launched WEWN short wave radio network in December of 1992.

In 1993, Mother announced that our community would return to wearing the full traditional habit. She decided that on Christmas Eve at Midnight Mass, the sisters would don the traditional veil for the first time. Sr. Raphael wrote "When all was completed, Mother Angelica and I finally stared at each other. I saw the Mother Angelica I first met in Canton, Ohio, and she saw me as I looked when she first began to teach me about Our Lord and His Love for me. We both began to laugh. The years fell away and we hugged each other like two old friends who had just run into each other again after many years."

She added, "There is an awe about being clothed in a habit that Jesus Himself has picked out for you. The sounds of the activity around you become silenced and you are enclosed in a tiny cloister within the cloister."

As the Network behind our Monastery continued to expand, Mother Angelica felt she had to make changes to protect the nuns' life of prayer and adoration. The Network was hiring more employees, more pilgrims were visiting the Network facilities, and at the same time the community was getting more vocations than the small Monastery could hold.

In 1995, Mother Angelica began searching for property in a quiet place away from all the noise of the world, desiring to set her community in a place more conducive to contemplation. She found a farm surrounded by a river situated about an hour drive north of Birmingham.

This same year, on June 2, Reverend Mother informed us that Sr. Raphael had cancer. On June 9, 1995, a surgeon removed the cancer, saying it was contained and that he did not feel it had spread anywhere else. Sr. Raphael recuperated normally from the surgery and resumed her normal religious life as Vicar of the community. She continued doing the things she enjoyed including artwork, needlepoint, writing and singing solos at Mass.

In 1996, Mother Angelica traveled to Colombia to raise funds and seek assistance for EWTN's Spanish programs. She was invited by Salesian Father Juan Pablo Rodriguez to attend Mass at the Sanctuary of the Divine Child Jesus in Bogotá. It was here that the statue of the Divine Child became alive, turned and spoke to her saying, "Build Me a temple and I will help those who help you." So what started out as a monastery farm chapel became a "temple for the Divine Child Jesus."

As Mother began building the chapel and then the Monastery surrounding it, she felt that it would be in some way a new beginning for our community in a more monastic atmosphere. She would give lessons to the nuns about the spiritual

renewal she desired for them. She emphasized that she wanted us to be a holy community of adorers of the Most Blessed
Sacrament. "Communal holiness is a power that cannot be contained to a place. It goes throughout the world. You have to be
aware of who you are—your great responsibility before God to
become holy!"

As Sr. Raphael listened to Mother's words, she was full of
enthusiasm for this fresh beginning. She began reading books
on the life and writings of St. Thérèse and developed a great
love for her. She spoke passionately about our life of adoration
and her desire to grow daily deeper in union with Jesus, her
beloved Spouse. She looked eagerly toward the day we would
move to the new Monastery and begin anew in that quiet, contemplative atmosphere, where she could sing His praises in the
beautiful new Temple as well as in the quiet beauty of His cre-
ation, among the trees and flowers in our cloistered gardens.
But our thoughts are not always His thoughts for us.

In May of 1999, just a few months before we were to move
to the new Monastery in Hanceville, Alabama, Sister Raphael
began feeling very exhausted. She was given test after test until
finally a CAT scan revealed that she had lymphoma—cancer.
Sr. Raphael somberly told one of the sisters that she had sat at
Mother's lessons for many years, and Mother had always taught
that "To love God is to love His Will." "I don't want to just accept this; I want to love it, because in loving His Will, I am
loving God."

A few weeks later, Sr. Raphael shared with us some thoughts
that were heavy on her heart, "things you think about when
you are near death. Little things—treasures the Lord asks us to
do." She gently encouraged us to always be faithful to the Rule,
and being more considerate to give Reverend Mother a little
quiet time. "That's all we have to give to God—our will and
our obedience." Sr. Raphael became choked up. Her love for

Reverend Mother was so great that her only concern was not for herself, but for Reverend Mother and the community and the holiness of each sister.

JESUS, THOU ART COMING...

The nuns moved into the new Monastery on December 3rd, 1999, and the Temple was solemnly dedicated on December 19th. Sr. Raphael attended the beautiful Mass in her wheel chair. She was never able to sing at the Conventual Mass in the new chapel. She was admitted to the hospital a few days before Christmas, and stayed there until January 5th, when she came home, knowing that she was dying.

As her death drew closer, Mother Angelica told the sisters: "Mother Vicar's death will be very hard on me. She's been a loyal, faithful friend all these years." She said Sr. Raphael would be coming home to die, but she had not complained even once. During this difficult time her greatest virtue has shown through: her nobility. Few people ever go from generosity to nobility, but Sr. Raphael did. It is easy to give away things, and that is generosity. However, it is difficult to give "self"—and that is nobility. The only thing that lasts from this world to the next is the heart of an adorer.

Early in the morning after she returned home, Sr. Raphael was wide awake, with big smiles. She said, "I'm so happy to die! I'm going home to Jesus!" That evening the sisters gathered around her bed and she began to sing. They joined in and sang many of their favorite songs. She told them that when she got to heaven she would sing her "highest note" for Jesus! This un-expected rallying was a great experience of healing and joy for the entire community.

On January 8, 2000, at 3:30 a.m., the nurse called Mother

Angelica from the infirmary and told her that Sr. Raphael's pulse was very erratic. By the time Reverend Mother arrived at her bedside, Sr. Raphael was talking, and said she saw two lights coming toward her—Jesus and Mary. "I see two lights— they are coming! O Jesus! My love—I love You! Yes, yes! I don't know why…yes, because He loves me so much! Mary! My Jesus! He's so beautiful! He's all Light!"

The nurses told us that Sr. Raphael had had no morphine since the previous night. Every time the nurse asked if she wanted some morphine, Sr. Raphael would reply, "No, I want to be alert."

Later that morning when Mother Angelica and some of the sisters were in her room, she said, "It's daylight, Mother." Mother responded: "He's coming…but He's slow." (Everyone laughed.) Then Sr. Raphael said, "O Mother, it's so beautiful! Thank you for everything! Everything you've told me is true! O yes, I hear that Voice. O Jesus, my beautiful Jesus!" Sr. Raphael's face was radiant and her eyes were sparkling with joy. "All the pain is over. We can all laugh together and sing together." "O, He's coming for me! Goodbye, my beautiful sisters! No fears… don't be afraid of death!"

On January 9th, Mother Angelica prayed the Litany of the Dying, the "Hail, Holy Queen" and made the Profession of Faith for Sr. Raphael, renewal of Vows, etc. Sr. Raphael said "Jesus" very softly. Then, "O my Jesus, help me, I love You. My Jesus…." Her eyes opened and closed. Barely audible, "Jesus, I love You."

Reverend Mother went over to the side of Sr. Raphael's bed and lowered the side rail, kissed her on the forehead, and whispered to her "It's OK." Sr. Raphael responded, "Mother, I love you." Her eyes were tearing. Reverend Mother patted her cheek and held her shoulder, encircling her head and shoulders in her arms. Sr. Raphael was trying to clear her throat. She said, "I love you." These were to be her last recognizable words. Sr. Raphael died with her Profession Crucifix in her hand. She died in the arms of our Abbess, Mother M. Angelica.

The Lord had been interiorly preparing her for this, as exactly the year before she died, she had been inspired to write one day after receiving Holy Communion:

> *To hear Your Voice, to see Your Eyes before me,*
> *To know the rapture of Your Love for me.*
> *My heart cries out to You, my only Treasure.*
> *My heart cries out, for all Eternity.*
>
> *What ecstasy awaits my path to You, Lord.*
> *I know I'll find You when Time ends for me.*
> *Then I will hear Your Footsteps drawing near me.*
> *You'll hurry to my arms, embracing me.*
>
> *Oh, all you Angels come to be my escort,*
> *Arriving at my birth, through life till death.*
> *You lead me on, inspiring me with courage*
> *And hope that I'll arrive to meet my Love*
> *To know my destiny, will ever be*
> *In His Blessed Company!*

The last two days of her life were like a Pentecost for her. Once Love had cast out all fear through the purification that was accomplished by her suffering, she manifested all seven Gifts of the Holy Spirit in such holy joy and exuberance that it was like a new Pentecost for us all.

Reverend Mother told the nuns, regarding Sr. Raphael's passing: "We don't know what wondrous things God will work through her death. Be thankful to God for everything. She suffered much during her whole life. None of you know, and you shouldn't. We don't know what she suffered from. In many ways, we are strangers, although we lived with her. She had great sufferings…. Only God knows what she suffered from and who she suffered for. We should all rejoice that, in the midst of tremendous pain, internal and external, she was able to say 'Yes!' to God to the end. May our end be as good and as holy…. Today have quiet joy and profound sorrow, that…" (Reverend Mother began to cry.) "I think she spent some days [staying here with us] more than she would have had to, and I know she's praying for all of us. Whatever we judge our lives by, let us judge by these last few days. Let us all say, 'Yes, Lord!' as she did, as Our Lady did, at least in our hearts."

Sr. Raphael's Inspirations

Letting the noise of the world go on around us and not allowing it to disturb our union with God in the depths of our souls is a secret of the spiritual life that escapes many people. Being silent and awestruck before God is a perfect prayer of praise. What can we add by words to His grandeur and majesty? Everything in nature proclaims His Greatness and Omnipotence. How does a moment go by that we could ever forget the One Who has provided for our every need? His Arms are always around us, His sweet Spirit is ever our model and example of life, and Jesus' holy Mother watches over us with tender love. "Where is there a people whose God is so near, as our God is near unto us?"

THE MORNING STAR

My Lady, my Lady, how beautiful you are!
   Your eyes are as resplendent, as is the Morning Star.
Your voice upon the meadowland is like a melody
   That wafts its way across the world—a melancholy plea:

"Behold, my children seeking, what will not satisfy.
   Their hearts are filled with fleeting joys, they do not hear my cry.
Oh, how I long to gather you, as mother hen her young.
   To hover gently over you until your song is sung.

Your life goes by so hastily, you take no time to hear
   The message of my dearest Son, that calls so loud and clear."
"Give Me your hearts, I've given Mine, My Love pours from the Cross.
   I paid so great a price for you, I cannot bear the loss.

My Mother gave Me Life and Birth. My Father sent Me here
   To make you all My brothers and sons of God so dear.
Why is it that you waver, in giving Me your all?
   I came so meek and humble and laid in cattle stall.

I did not come to frighten you, but to invite your love.
   I left My Father's Bosom, My Home in Heaven above.
I call you in so many ways—the beauty of the sea,
   The bird calls and the budding spring—created all by Me.

All these cry out and witness to a Love that never dies,
   But wait to welcome when you make your journey to the skies.

Then take My Hand, come walk with Me, the way I choose to go.
  I have a plan made out for you, your destiny to show.

Forget the world's allurements, these shadows that betray.
  They promise you great happiness, while leading you astray.
Come, find your safety in My Heart, away from earthly charms.
  Come, hasten, child, the way is clear. I'll hold you in My Arms."

~ Sr. Mary Raphael, PCPA

He [God] is so close and so mysterious. His ways are not our ways but they do their purifying work in our lives even though we don't often understand. If Our Lady's statue came alive and she were here beside my cart, talking to me, what would she say? "Trust my Son. His ways are more sure than yours. His plans for you are beyond your comprehension. Your dreams are only a shadow of His dreams for you. When the time is right you will understand. Bow to His Will and accept whatever He allows to happen to you. Surrender everything to Him. He will never leave you alone. You will not be disappointed."

Mass begins and I think of all the angels that fill the Chapel to adore Our Lord. They are singing with us and we with them and I feel enveloped in their presence. Receiving Jesus in Holy Communion is the climax of every Mass. What a Gift. Our God lives in us. I ask Our Lady to cradle him first in her heart before He comes into mine and then I place all my love, sorrows, guilt, bungling and many failures into His Heart to be burned in the fire of His Love.

Mother Vicar -

    An obedient daughter, a loyal & faithful friend, a joyful spouse of Christ.

                       -Mother M. Angelica

I THIRST

My God, how often have I turned away from You
  How often tried to quell Your whispered word.
The more I fled away—the more I felt You near
  Pleading, waiting, asking to be heard.

"Lord of the Universe"—was not enough for You
  Great as was the title, yet I knew
Holding sway and being "Master of my 'heart'"
  Was a conquest that meant more to you.

How I longed for peace and yet, made war with Peace,
  Striving to be free—to break this chain.
Attracted by a love that was too great for me,
  Quivering in separation's pain.

All or nothing was the challenge You would fling.
  You had given all that Love could give.
On the cross Your Life's blood had flowed out for me.
  You had tasted Death that I might live.

Lesser loves I sought to take the place of Yours.
  Could earth's beauty, music, friendship—last?
Once I'd wrest my heart from out Your wounded Hands,
  Could I face what "might have been"—and passed?

Where is love to equal what You offered me?
  Nothing in the world is worth a soul.
Whither hast Thou fled, Beloved, answer me?
  Come and shake the anguish of my soul.

Now that I would seek Thee, Thou art hid from me.
  Will this yearning for You not be stilled?
Is this thirst the answer to Your Love's Demands?
  Will I ever drink and not be filled?

                                  ~ *Sr. Mary Raphael, PCPA*

Love Jesus—His Heart is wounded by these blasphemous times—hold His Head against your heart and comfort Him. He loves you so much.

Imagine being thought of by God before time began. What love He had for you and me! He determined all our ancestors up to our conception so that we would be who we are and what we will become. He called us by name. He chose us to be! Greater than this was the love that impelled Him to send His own Son through His most perfect creature—Mary, the Mother of Jesus.

The Heavenly Father describes Himself in Isaiah 40:11. "He (Yahweh) is like a shepherd feeding His flock, gathering lambs in His Arms, holding them against His Breast and leading to their rest the mother ewes." What a tender Father who looks on us with such caring and concern. No wonder that Jesus, too, would call Himself the Good Shepherd, since He did only what He saw the Father do.

Sister M. Raphael

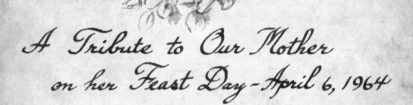

A Tribute to Our Mother on her Feast Day – April 6, 1964

Can you tell us, Little Mother,
  Why it's springtime every day?
Why our hearts are filled with gladness
  As we go along our way?

There is joy in every sunrise.
  There is happiness to spare.
Laughter spills out through our cloister
  Into souls all filled with care.

Eyes look bright and heart-beats quicken
  As from out the parlor grate
Come your words of love and comfort
  To dispel all fear and hate.

O your love for your Creator
  Is a real and vital thing.
And His Presence on our altar
  Where He reigns here as our King.

Is the source of all your courage.
  He's the Spark that lights the Fire
Of the burning love within you
  That compels your one desire.

O, that souls would seek for Union
  As they seek for lesser things;
Speak to Him as loving children;
  Learn the happiness it brings

To belong to such a Father.
  And to realize that He hears
Every plea and every heartache
  We have told Him through the years.

There's a reason, Little Mother,
  That our hearts would rest awhile
In the warmth of your example.
  In the comfort of your smile;

Why we find the sweet contagion
  Of your unassuming way
Shining for us as a beacon
  Changing darkness into day.

For the light that shines within you
  Tells us Jesus is your own;
That your soul is His pure Chapel,
  And your heart His glowing Throne.

And the building of this trysting place
   Was mightier in scope,
Took more tears and love and sorrow,
   Took more fiercely burning hope;

Took more time and more devotion
   And fulfillment of your dreams,
Than the pouring of the mortar
   And the setting of the beams.

In this cloister of Our Lady,
   Where you labored without rest
To prepare a worthy dwelling
   For our Consecrated Guest;

Where He rules our little family,
   Through your gentleness and love
As He uses all your efforts
   To direct our thoughts above.

As we mark your second Feast Day
   And your daughters gather 'round
We would like to whisper, "Thank you,"
   For the happiness we've found.

And we pray each coming Feast Day
   Finds us nearer to our goal,
More united to our Master,
   More a Family—heart and soul.

~ Sr. Mary Raphael, PCPA

Jesus is the Divine Artist. We only see part of the picture He is working on. We can't see what is in His Mind or what He is creating with the materials of our lives. We need only to yield to Him for He is the Master and the Artist. He uses the brush to paint the canvas. He is at work in ways we least expect. The picture in our thinking and the work in which He is engaged are entirely different. He makes no idle strokes. He is never mixing colors out of idle curiosity. His every move is of vital creativity and every stroke is part of a whole. Never be dismayed or alarmed. Say to your questioning heart, "He does all things well. He is the Infinite Beloved of my soul."

The Heart of Jesus reaches out to us for comfort in these times of so much unrest, unhappiness and sin. Why don't we run after Him as He runs after us? He has everything worthwhile to offer us and the world has only deception and false principles. He is the only One we can trust with our lives, our joys and our sorrows. His Hand is always reaching out to us. When a soul and God finally separate, God's is the last Hand to lose its hold.

Sr. M. Raphael

Do you notice when you pray that your thoughts often tend to wash up onto the shores of yesterday or roll out onto the ocean of tomorrow, leaving the precious present moment and its graces abandoned on the rocks? This is the sad plight of many of our prayers but we need gently to bring our thoughts back to the precious Now, which is all that is within our reach. Jesus, with His Love and gifting, waits in the present moment (the only time we have) to get our attention so He can speak to us, if we but listen to His gentle Voice and learn the lessons He is teaching us.

ETERNITY

You, You alone I love now and forever.
  All other loves are gathered in the Tide
That follows me and yet goes on before me,
  All sweep together and in You abide.

How can I know that You are always with me?
  I see Your Eyes in each and everyone who walks beside me.
I follow all the Saints who trod before me,
  And those who come behind will pray for me, for all Eternity.

My life I give to You, my dearest Savior,
  You clasp me by the hand and guide me on.
Your Presence comforts me and goes before me
  In all my trials until Eternity.

Come, let me hear Your Voice upon the thunder.
  The mountains glow with fire, Your Spirit comes
To lead me safe to You, My God forever,
  My God, my Everything Eternally.

I see Your Face reflected in the Heavens,
  As clouds portend Your stride from Heaven to earth.
My Father, God, my truest Love, my Jesus,
  I long to be with You Eternally

To hear Your Voice, to see Your Eyes before me,
  To know the rapture of Your Love for me.
My heart cries out to You, my only Treasure.
  My heart cries out, for all Eternity.

What ecstasy awaits my path to You, Lord.
  I know I'll find You when Time ends for me.
Then I will hear Your Footsteps drawing near me.
  You'll hurry to my arms, embracing me.

Oh, all you Angels come to be my escort,
  Arriving at my birth, through life till death.
You lead me on, inspiring me with courage
  And hope that I'll arrive to meet my Love.

To know my destiny, will ever be
  In His Blessed Company!

~ Sr. Mary Raphael, PCPA

We need to get engrossed in the saying of the Rosary every day. It is a great comfort to reflect on the highlights of the lives of Jesus and Mary, from the Angel Gabriel's announcement of the Birth of Jesus to the Coronation of Our Lady as Queen of the Angels. We can walk in Mary's footsteps and see Jesus through her eyes, sharing the joys, sorrows and glorious mysteries of their lives. Please do not neglect this treasure. Rather than complain about the times we live in, we need to do something about it and send our "Hail Mary's" to heaven to placate the displeasure of God.

Each morning we wake up to a new chance at life, a new opportunity to serve our great God in our little ways. What promise each day brings of new surprises and signs of His immense Love for us. Everything in nature has its source and purpose in Him. The sound of birds calling, the draft of breezes that caress our faces, the life-giving air we breathe, are all gifts from Him. Why is it that we always know Spring will burst out each year in all her colors and enchant our hearts? What mysterious movements of the earth let the dusk overtake us each night and make morning break with such splashes of color across the sky? What secret timing brings the fish to their feeding grounds and directs flocks of birds to their Winter sanctuaries?

Our universe is God's timepiece that He created and fondles in His Hand as a treasure into which He sent His Divine Son and His Son's holy Mother. How important we are to Him!

The hardships in our lives, though not always ordained by God, are nevertheless permitted by Him for a great good—our sanctification. Since all things of this world quickly pass away, His work in our lives is to emphasize the eternal truths—His Love, His Church, the Sacraments and the graces of the Present Moment in which lie the seeds of our holiness according to how we respond to His inspirations.

GOING HOME

Remember when we used to ride in the country and see yellow fields with rows of hay piled up like Indian teepees along the road and huge orange pumpkins scattered among them? The air was brisk and clean, and great, puffy clouds were making their slow procession across the sky. Trees were turning riotous colors—rust, red, yellow, gold, orange, and some still green. Farmers were selling the last of their produce and apple cider began appearing on the table.

One day like this in Ohio, I looked out the window and huge snow flakes were drifting down and getting caught in the bright-colored foliage. It was time to get out our roller skates and find a hill that we could sail down from.

I wonder if stepping from our earthly home into Eternity is something like this. After a life of activity mixed with prayer, will we be excited about going Home to our Heavenly Father? Will we be ready to leave the battlefield of life and head out for a high hill where Jesus is waiting for us?

When you hear about after-death experiences you wonder if you will be carried through the tunnel of Purgatory toward the light, or will Jesus be waiting there in your room to take you in His Arms and press you to His Sacred Heart? Will Our Lady be there with her beautiful smile as our Guardian Angel stands at attention, waiting to greet you?

We will be carried by our very own True Love to the Throne of our Father. "It is You, O Lord, Who have accomplished all we have done."

~ Sr. Mary Raphael, PCPA